Love you
forever,

Mom &
Dad

# ONE-MINUTE
# *Devotions*
# *for* COUPLES

## BOB & CHERYL
# MOELLER

**HARVEST HOUSE PUBLISHERS**
EUGENE, OREGON

*Cover design by Koechel Peterson & Associates, Inc., Minneapolis, Minnesota*
*Cover photo © Ron Chapple Studios / Thinkstock*
*The authors are represented by MacGregor Literary, Inc., of Hillsboro, Oregon*

---

To our friend and editor, Rod Morris,
whom God used to change the course of our ministry
two decades ago. For Better, For Worse, For Keeps
Ministries began the day you called and invited us to submit a
book proposal on marriage. Thank you ever so much.

Congratulations, Rod and Deanne,
on your thirty-fifth wedding anniversary.

---

**ONE-MINUTE DEVOTIONS FOR COUPLES**
Copyright © 2013 by Bob and Cheryl Moeller
Published by Harvest House Publishers
Eugene, Oregon 97402
www.harvesthousepublishers.com

ISBN 978-0-7369-5203-3 (pbk.)
ISBN 978-0-7369-5204-0 (eBook)

**Printed in China**

13 14 15 16 17 18 19 20 21 22 / RDS-CD / 10 9 8 7 6 5 4 3 2 1

# A WORD *to the* READER

If we were selling marriage insurance, the only policy we would offer would contain just four words, "Prayer and God's Word."

Nothing we know of can better safeguard and protect your marriage bond than coming together daily in prayer and the study of the holy Scriptures. As you call on your heavenly Father together, you gain the incredible assurance that He hears you, "for where two or three gather in my name, there am I with them" (Matthew 18:20). As you fill your hearts and minds with the Scriptures, you gain the powerful confidence He is at work in your lives, for God declared through the prophet Isaiah:

> "So is my word that goes out from my mouth:
> It will not return to me empty,
> but will accomplish what I desire
> and achieve the purpose for which I sent it."
> (Isaiah 55:11)

That's why we've put together these 250 one-minute devotionals for you to use each day as a couple. We want you to taste of the power, love, and joy that can be yours when you call on the name of the Lord in prayer and study His flawless Word together.

Our prayer is that the Lord will use your daily devotional time together to build a hedge around your marriage so high, so wide, and so deep that nothing will ever get through to compromise your vows. It is God's express will that what He has joined together no one ever separate. In Jesus you can experience the love and strength to remain faithful and committed to each other for a lifetime: "A cord of three strands is not quickly broken" (Ecclesiastes 4:12).

Remember, your marriage is for better, for worse, and for keeps.

Love in Christ,
Bob and Cheryl

> *"I will give you a new heart and put a new*
> *spirit in you; I will remove from you your*
> *heart of stone and give you a heart of flesh."*

 EZEKIEL 36:26

Does your marriage need a heart transplant?
The prophet Ezekiel made a remarkable promise regarding the transforming love of God. Regardless of how troubled our marriage may have been up to now, God can take our heart of stone and replace it with a heart of flesh. It begins with trusting the heart of God, who has revealed Himself in Jesus Christ and His finished work on the Cross. There, bearing our sins, Jesus opened a source of love that can literally transform our life. If our heart is stone cold, we need to ask God to perform a heart transplant—to replace the old one with a new one that is once again soft and tender toward our spouse.

> *Heavenly Father, if my heart has started to*
> *harden toward those I love the most, I ask You*
> *to do what only You can do—to restore it to*
> *a soft and caring heart—a heart like Yours. I*
> *ask this in the name of Jesus. Amen.*

*Dear friends, let us love one another, for love
comes from God…This is love: not that we loved
God, but that he loved us and sent his Son as an
atoning sacrifice for our sins. Dear friends, since
God so loved us, we also ought to love one another.*

1 John 4:7,10-11

What's the source of all love in our marriages?

The great missionary David Livingstone launched
an expedition to find the source of the magnificent Nile
River in Africa. Have we ever asked, what is the source of
true love in our marriage? Is it our romantic attraction? Is
it our compatible personality traits? Or is the origin of true
love found outside the two of us?

Today's Scripture teaches us that all genuine love
comes from God. Fortunately we don't have to attend a
seminar, buy a DVD series, or make an exotic safari to discover its transforming power. We simply have to ask God
for it. Since God's love is the true source of all love, why
not invite that river to flow into our marriage?

*Dear God, let the inexhaustible river of Your
love cascade through our marriage. Amen.*

*Search me, God, and know my heart;*
*test me and know my anxious thoughts.*
*See if there is any offensive way in me,*
*and lead me in the way everlasting.*

PSALM 139:23-24

If our marriage is going to change, who should make the first move?

A twentieth-century devotional writer tells of a couple that never agreed on what to listen to on their radio. One day the wife realized the arguing in their marriage was due mainly to selfish issues in her own heart. She surprised her husband by switching the station to what he liked.

"Why did you just do that?" he asked.

"Because I know it's what you prefer," she calmly replied.

He got up and turned it to back to her music. From that point onward, the acrimony and fighting in their marriage began to dissipate. One person took the first step of letting God examine their heart and make changes. Our marriage doesn't usually change when our spouse changes; change typically begins when we make the first move of letting God remove any offensive way in us.

*Dear Lord, You have our permission here and*
*now to examine our hearts and to take away*
*anything that displeases You. Amen.*

*I pray that out of his glorious riches he may strengthen*
*you with power through his Spirit in your inner being,*
*so that Christ may dwell in your hearts through faith.*

EPHESIANS 3:16-17

If we wanted the soul of a loving person, whose heart
would we ask for?

Someone once said that if we want the soul of a musi-
cian, we should ask for the heart of Beethoven. If we want
the soul of a sculptor, ask for the heart of Michelangelo.
But if we wanted the soul of a loving person, whose heart
would we ask for?

First and last on the list should be the heart of Jesus
Christ. But to receive a new heart from God we must take
a step of faith. We ask Jesus Christ to forgive our sin and
wrongdoing, and then accept His free offer of grace. We
trust Him alone for our eternal reconciliation with God.
Once we've taken those steps, we will now have the soul of
a loving husband or wife. Why? Our heart will beat with
the very heart of Christ.

*Lord Jesus, today I place all my trust in the*
*finished work of the cross for my salvation,*
*and I invite You to dwell in my heart forever*
*through faith. Amen.*

*He who finds a wife finds what is good*
*and receives favor from the LORD.*

PROVERBS 18:22

Have you been emotional window-shopping lately? People in struggling marriages sometimes use fantasy as a means of escaping the difficult realities of their unhappy lives. They see an attractive person and think, *I know I'd be happy with him (or her)*. They end up refusing to invest the needed time and energy in their relationship because their thoughts are always directed toward someone else.

It's only when we come to the point where we stop such emotional window-shopping and decide to celebrate the choice we made on our wedding day that our feelings of joy and gratitude begin to flow back into our lives. We need to come to the realization where we say, "If I'm to enjoy my marriage, it will be with the person God has given me. They are a living example of the favor of God in my life."

Once we reaffirm that good purchase, we'll never go shopping again.

*Lord Jesus, allow me to see my partner for the*
*gift they are to my life. Let me each day express*
*my thanksgiving that they are a living*
*example of Your favor. Amen.*

*"If they obey and serve Him,
they will spend the rest of their days in prosperity
and their years in contentment."*

Job 36:11

Wat does it take to be content in marriage?
We attended a banquet one evening where one of the men at the head table was obviously flirting with a younger woman seated next to him. He didn't realize anyone else would notice his behavior, but we watched with sadness as he ignored his wife to spend the entire evening talking to the other woman.

Unless we are firmly committed to the principle that our spouse comes first in our lives after our relationship with Jesus Christ, we will likely become prisoners of perpetual distraction. We can even make fools of ourselves in front of other people. The good news is that God has designed our emotions to respond to the willful decisions we make. If we make a conscious decision to be contented with the person we married, and entertain no other offers, we will eventually find true fulfillment with that person.

*Heavenly Father, help us to put our spouse
before all others. Help us to focus on their
strengths, virtues, and talents, not on their
shortcomings or weaknesses. Let us experience
true contentment. Amen.*

*But godliness with contentment is great gain.*

1 Timothy 6:6

After-dinner mint, anyone?

For several years we drove a second car we affectionately called our "After-Dinner Mint." Why? The manufacturer had painted it a yellow-green, like the color found in chocolate mint wafers you get at a nice restaurant after dinner. It was often hard to pull up next to an expensive foreign car in our odd-colored vehicle, but when we added up the cost of buying another car, complete with tax, title, and stickers, the After-Dinner Mint started tasting much better. Once we decide to be content with what we have, we actually can find delight in it.

When it comes to marriage, we need to make a similar decision and say, "I choose here and now to remain married to my spouse for the rest of my life, and I will not even consider any other alternative." We need to continually rehearse in our minds the real value of remaining true, faithful, and thankful for the person we are married to. Such a godly decision will bring great gain and leave a sweet taste to our marriage.

*Lord Jesus, create in us a heart of thankful
contentment for each other. Amen.*

*In this same way, husbands ought to love their wives as
their own bodies. He who loves his wife loves himself.*

EPHESIANS 5:28

W hat's the order of priorities in your life?

Al, a friend who was an officer in the military,
told us that whenever he would return from active duty
overseas, he would first meet his wife, Diane, alone for a
day (leaving the children with proper child-care), then
come home to greet his children.

That's the high priority we need to give to our husbands or wives. We must choose to make our marriage
the most important relationship in our lives. This means
putting our husband or wife above our relatives, parents,
coworkers, and even children. Our order of relationship
priorities in life must be God first, our spouse second, our
children third, and then others take their place in line
after that. Our relationship with our spouse must take
precedence over time spent on the phone with other family members, rounds of golf with clients, and even Little
League games coaching our kids.

We must learn to love our spouse as we love ourselves.

*Heavenly Father, help us this day to put first
things first after Christ—starting with our
relationship with our spouse. Amen.*

*Sarah lived to be a hundred and twenty-seven years*
*old. She died…in the land of Canaan, and Abraham*
*went to mourn for Sarah and to weep over her.*

GENESIS 23:1-2

Do you appreciate the person you are married to today?
Charles Swindoll once said that he's attended
more than one funeral where the husband wept on his
shoulder and said, "I never knew what I really had until
she was gone." We must not let that happen in our life. We
should not wait until it's too late to make our marriage the
priority it needs to be in our life.

How do we learn to truly appreciate our spouse? It
begins by treating them as if they are the most important
person in our lives. We need to talk to them frequently
throughout the day, think about them often when we're
away, and say no to some commitments just so the two of
us can spend time together.

The more we invest in each other, the more we will
appreciate our husband or wife.

*Our Lord Jesus, teach us today to see how pre-*
*cious life is and how quickly time passes. Help*
*us to appreciate the time we have together as a*
*gift to be valued. Amen.*

*"'For this reason a man will leave his father
and mother and be united to his wife, and
the two will become one flesh.' So they are no
longer two, but one flesh. Therefore what God
has joined together, let no one separate."*

MARK 10:7-9

Who gets more of your attention—your spouse or your children?

We are given children for only a few short years. It's in the scheme of things that our kids will one day grow up, leave home, and bond to another person in marriage. But that's why we are given a lifelong mate, so that when this inevitable separation from our offspring occurs, we will not be left alone. The strength of our marriage, if it has been a top priority, will be adequate to meet the needs of both of us when left with an empty nest.

Stop and evaluate today who gets the majority of our time and attention. Is it our kids, who will be gone in a certain number of years, or our spouse, who God may give us for the rest of our life (if they should live that long)?

*Our Blessed Creator, let no one separate what
You have joined together—not even our dear
children. Amen.*

*Remember how fleeting is my life.*
*For what futility you have created all humanity!*

Psalm 89:47

Which wall is your ladder leaning against?

We live in a busy culture—too busy at times. We should work to live; we should not live to work. Spouses who spend their lives giving their best shot to their career often make a sad discovery as they grow older. Though they've reached the top of the success ladder, it's leaning against the wrong wall.

A successful businessman once refused to participate in a heart disease reduction program at work. "Why would I want to live longer?" he said. "I have only a banking relationship with my family."

Choosing to make our marriage and children our priority may be difficult if we've been accustomed to giving our best to our work. But we can discover a brand-new level of joy and intimacy in life when we lean our ladder against the right wall—a fulfilling marriage and family life. One way to start moving the ladder today is to remember how quickly life goes by. It is indeed here today and gone tomorrow.

*Dear God, teach us to value the fulfilling over*
*the fleeting starting this very day. Amen.*

*For God so loved the world that he gave his
one and only Son, that whoever believes in
him shall not perish but have eternal life.*

JOHN 3:16

Is love more what we do than what we say?

We heard a family seminar speaker once make this simple but profound statement: "Love is action." He was so right. The words "I love you" are easy to say but so difficult to do. Love is the willingness to do for our spouse many of the things that don't come naturally to us—such as forgiving, serving, or complimenting them.

We have several all-talk radio stations in our city. Twenty-four hours a day you can hear nothing but talk. Let's commit ourselves to becoming more than all-talk radio when it comes to loving our spouse. God went far beyond talking to demonstrate His love for us—He gave His one and only Son.

Don't forget love is not what we say, or intend to do, but what we actually do.

*O Loving God, we thank You that Your love
for us went far beyond words, but went all the
way to the cross of Jesus Christ. May we follow
that example of love. Amen.*

*Love is patient, love is kind. It does not envy, it
does not boast, it is not proud. It does not
dishonor others, it is not self-seeking, it is not
easily angered, it keeps no record of wrongs.*

1 CORINTHIANS 13:4-5

What is the best way to say I love you?

One popular brand of athletic shoes was made famous by their slogan, "Just do it." When it comes to love, there's certainly no substitute for actually doing something loving. What's the alternative? To stay distant, demand other people make the first move, and spend the rest of our life in loneliness and isolation, all just to make a point?

Love is doing for the other person all the things our selfish human nature doesn't want to do. It's leaving them the last piece of pizza or willingly spending time with their difficult relatives during the holidays. It's all the small ways we can say, "I love you more than I love me."

Let's really love our spouse and watch how much of the other aspects of our relationship take care of themselves.

*Dear Jesus, give us an opportunity today to do
something loving for each other and keep us
from self-seeking. Amen.*

*Do nothing out of selfish ambition or vain
conceit. Rather, in humility value others above
yourselves, not looking to your own interests
but each of you to the interests of others.*

PHILIPPIANS 2:3-4

Do we need some of heaven on earth in our marriage?
We once read of a Hollywood celebrity who claimed the most important person in our lives ought to be ourselves. Ultimately, the starlet said, we spend all day with ourselves, we eat with ourselves, and we go to bed with ourselves. Her remarks truly fit the narcissistic spirit of our age. But they are pathetically misinformed.

If the most important person in our lives is ourselves, we will never know true love or intimacy. Giving, not taking, is love's secret. Someone said the difference between heaven and hell is that in heaven people serve each other, while in hell everyone wants to be served.

The same could be said of marriage. We will experience some of heaven on earth when we begin to look to our spouse's interests, not just our own.

*Lord Jesus, put to death the selfish nature in
our lives so that Your nature can make us
servants of one another. Amen.*

*"For I know the plans I have for you," declares
the LORD, "plans to prosper you and not to harm
you, plans to give you hope and a future."*

JEREMIAH 29:11

Does God have an amazing plan for our marriage?
For years Campus Crusade for Christ has used a small booklet titled "The Four Spiritual Laws" to lead people to faith in Christ. The first principle is that God loves us and has a wonderful plan for our life.

That foundational truth also applies to our marriage. We need to believe not only that God has a purpose but that He has an extraordinary one for our marriage. That means that nothing in our relationship ever catches God by surprise. No trauma, no heartache, and no disappointment escape His notice. If we commit our marriage to Jesus Christ, we can be certain He will use every event, good or bad, for our good and His glory. Given adequate time and distance, we will see just how God's plan unfolded in a beautiful way in our marriage.

*Lord Jesus, even though our days are
sometimes difficult, and many of our
questions remain unanswered, help us to
place our complete trust in Your extraordinary
plan for our lives. Amen.*

*May your fountain be blessed,*
*and may you rejoice in the wife of your youth.*

PROVERBS 5:18

Do we celebrate or grieve the fact we got married?
We were part of a church volleyball game one Saturday afternoon when the match was suddenly interrupted by the loud noise and celebration of a wedding entourage driving past. Horns blared, streamers flapped, and attendants waved their arms from shining white limousines. "You poor fool," the man next to me muttered, unaware that anyone was listening. "You have no idea what you're getting yourself into."

What a tragic commentary (apparently) on his own marriage. The Bible teaches we are to respond just the opposite—we are to rejoice in the wife of our youth. If we can keep that perspective before us, we can live with the imperfections, failings, and faults in our spouse yet celebrate the precious person God gave us for a mate.

Next time we see a wedding entourage drive by, let's stop and celebrate the gift God gave us. It's a sure sign that His approval rests on our life.

*Dear Jesus, may both of us rejoice in*
*the partner of our youth for as long*
*as we both shall live. Amen.*

*In the heavens God has pitched a tent for the sun.*
*It is like a bridegroom coming out of his chamber,*
*like a champion rejoicing to run his course.*

PSALM 19:4-5

Did we marry to be miserable?

Every time we meet individuals going through a divorce, who have fallen into adultery, or who simply hate being married, we're reminded this isn't likely what they had in mind that beautiful Saturday afternoon they said their vows. As they dressed in elegant formal wear and sipped punch surrounded by friends and family, they never dreamed life would turn out to be such misery.

No, none of us married to be miserable, and if we find ourselves in that condition, we need to go to work on restoring our marriage today. God's intention is that we meet each day of our marriage with the joy of a bridegroom as he emerges to meet his bride. Let's recommit ourselves to our wedding vows, look for ways to show our spouse true love, and give up our self-focus and complaining heart—and say good-bye to our misery.

*Our heavenly Father, help us to remember*
*each morning the love that drew us to each*
*other the day we married—and rejoice. Amen.*

*All the days ordained for me were written in your book*
*before one of them came to be.*

PSALM 139:16

Who has the authority to say our marriage was a mistake?

From time to time we meet people who sincerely believe their marriage was a huge error. If we believe that about our marriage, on what authority can we say our marriage should never have been? Is it because our emotions tell you so? Is it because our mother thinks our mate is a disappointment? Did someone tell us that we need to leave the marriage to find the happiness we deserve?

We urge you to consider this question: Does God think your marriage was a big mistake? The Scriptures clearly tell us God is involved in our lives from day one, and that all the days were written before we were born. His plan has been in effect long before we said "I do."

We need to trust that even our marriage—difficult as it may be at the moment—is in His loving plan for our lives.

*Dear Jesus, thank You that from the very*
*beginning You have been involved in our lives*
*and our relationship. Thank You that You*
*don't make mistakes. Let us live by this faith.*
*Amen.*

*For our light and momentary troubles are achieving
for us an eternal glory that far outweighs them all.*

2 CORINTHIANS 4:17

Can our difficulties someday become precious to us?
A famous writer said something to this effect:
"Someday, given enough time, we will look back on
our lives and discover the most difficult moments have
become the most precious to us."

He was not saying that pain is itself precious or that
heartbreaking events should be seen as welcome events in
our lives. Rather, even in marriage's most stressful hours, if
we turn to each other rather than on each other, and look
to Jesus for our strength, we will someday discover the
incredible value and enduring blessing that comes from
facing life's adversity together.

It will undoubtedly take time, but we will eventually
see more clearly how God was at work in our troubles and
difficulties. The end result will be a spirit of thankfulness
even for the hours where it seemed there was apparently
nothing to thank God for.

*Lord Jesus, the tragedy of the cross was turned
to the victory of the resurrection. Help us to
believe even our worst hours can one day be
transformed into glorious thanksgiving as we
experience Your deliverance. Amen.*

*A friend loves at all times,*
*and a brother is born for a time of adversity.*

PROVERBS 17:17

On our fiftieth anniversary what memories will we cherish?

Ask a couple that's made it to the half-century mark, and they'll no doubt tell you about some of the grim years along the way. The time the husband lost his job, or one of their children died at birth, or a close family member was struck down with a serious disease. But if we watch closely, particularly the way they look into each other's eyes, we'll probably catch a glimpse of the deep understanding and love that exists between them.

The deep bonds of friendship in marriage are forged more in adversity than blessing. The result is an unspoken tie and connection that exists between a husband and a wife who have weathered the storms of life and emerged more committed to one another and to God.

If we reach our fiftieth anniversary, we will understand how much our spouse—our best friend—was born for adversity.

*Dear God, we know that the seas You have*
*given us have not always been calm, but*
*thank You that in the midst of the storms, we*
*have had You and each other. Amen.*

*With the tongue we praise our Lord and*
*Father, and with it we curse human beings,*
*who have been made in God's likeness…*
*My brothers and sisters, this should not be.*

JAMES 3:9-10

Is our sharp tongue cutting the fabric of our marriage?

To avoid doing lasting damage in our marriage with our words, we should remember several principles. First, we should ask God daily to set a guard over the door of our lips. Let the restraining work of the Holy Spirit keep us from uttering worthless words. Second, say nothing unless we know we are in control of our emotions. Strong emotions usually pass within eight minutes, so hold that thought until we are back in control. Third, imagine our words being remembered forever. Would we want them inscribed in granite for time immemorial? Fourth, think of our mate with the heart of a child. Would we speak in such a harsh way to a tender toddler?

Finally, we should memorize Scripture to remind ourselves that our tongue was made to praise our Lord and Father and to bless those made in His image.

*Dear Jesus, let us remember that the tears we*
*cause in another's eyes by our hurtful words*
*may reflect the tears in God's eyes. Amen.*

*But for that very reason I was shown mercy so that in
me, the worst of sinners, Christ Jesus might display
his immense patience as an example for those who
would believe in him and receive eternal life.*

1 Timothy 1:16

Can God use an imperfect marriage?

Let's face it. None of us is perfect, nor is our marriage. But does that mean God cannot use us to accomplish His perfect will? We can find encouragement by going back to the family tree of Jesus. His genealogy through Joseph and Mary reads in some cases like a gossip tabloid. There you discover adulterers, prostitutes, idol-worshippers, murderers, and more. Why would God print such embarrassing information?

Those names are there to make the point that God specializes in accomplishing His perfect purposes using imperfect people. The doctrine of grace teaches us God will fulfill His will through people like us, who have often messed up or made some major bad choices. We can find encouragement today knowing God can and will use our marriage regardless of our shortcomings.

*Lord Jesus, thank You perfection is no require-
ment for service in Your kingdom. You lived a
perfect life so that we don't have to.
Thank You so much. Amen.*

*Therefore let everyone who is godly pray to you…*
*You are my hiding place;*
*you will protect me from trouble*
*and surround me with songs of deliverance.*

PSALM 32:6-7

Have you and your spouse discovered a hiding place? Growing up in the Midwest, we remember the power and sometimes even the terror of turbulent springtime weather. Colliding air masses produced loud thunderstorms, driving rain, and even killer tornadoes. During one such terrible storm, our family was forced to huddle in the basement an entire night as tornadoes repeatedly touched down, wreaking havoc in our city. We remember the comfort, however, in knowing our family had a safe, secure hiding place to ride out the storm.

Life produces storms of all kinds. Every married couple needs a place of refuge where we can cling to God and ride out the wind and the turbulence together until it subsides. When storms hit in life, don't just head for the basement. Head first for God.

*Almighty God, we thank You that in the midst*
*of the most raging and terrifying storms of life,*
*there is a place where we can go to find refuge*
*and peace. Thank You that You are that*
*hiding place. Amen.*

*Blessed is the one whose sin the Lord
does not count against them
and in whose spirit is no deceit.*

Psalm 32:2

W hat is life's greatest blessing?

Here's a challenge for us as married couples: write down a list of life's top five blessings. We would imagine they might contain such good things as marriage, good health, children, and close friends. But what does the Bible say life's greatest blessing is?

The psalmist David answers this question: it is to experience the total and complete forgiveness of our sins. That and that alone assures our final salvation. Through the New Testament message, we know this salvation is accomplished through the death and resurrection of Jesus Christ. He opens the doors of eternal life to each of us who believe.

If you have not already experienced this blessing, it can be yours today. Simply ask the Lord Jesus for life's greatest gift—and it will be yours.

*Dear Lord Jesus, thank You for the incredible
offer of the complete forgiveness of our sins.
We accept that offer to place our faith
in You and in the pardon You purchased with
Your blood on the cross. By faith through
grace we believe we have now passed from
death to life. Amen.*

*If we confess our sins, he is faithful and
just and will forgive us our sins and
purify us from all unrighteousness.*

1 John 1:9

Whatever happened to sin?

Years ago a famous psychiatrist wrote a book titled *Whatever Became of Sin?* After treating people for a variety of emotional and mental disorders, he came to the firm conclusion the majority of his patients could go home if they just knew one thing—they were forgiven.

In marriage we often tend to blame the problems in our relationship on poor communication, lack of empathy, and a difficult childhood. There are no doubt elements of truth in each explanation, but we may be overlooking the most basic cause—our sin. We and our spouse may have acted in ways that offend God and that wound each other. The only remedy for sin is to confess, forsake, and renounce it. Then we can return to living rightly with God and each other.

When asked, "Whatever became of sin?" our answer will be, "Christ has forgiven it and taken it away."

*Lord Jesus, we confess the root problem in life
and relationships is sinful pride. Please forgive
us, cleanse us, and purify us from all
unrighteousness. Amen.*

*The acts of the flesh are obvious: sexual
immorality, impurity and debauchery; idolatry
and witchcraft; hatred, discord, jealousy, fits
of rage, selfish ambition, dissensions, factions
and envy; drunkenness, orgies, and the like.*

GALATIANS 5:19-21

D oes one size sin fit all?

We listened to a spokesperson for the American Cancer Society who once explained there are over two hundred varieties of the deadly disease. Great strides have been made in preventing and curing the malady, yet researchers agree the dozens of varieties of cancers require that each one be recognized separately.

In our marriages, sins of various types and varieties can attack our relationship. Jealousy, bitterness, anger, envy, lust, unfaithfulness, and others can threaten the life of our marriage covenant. In each case we need to define exactly what we are battling, admit it for what it is, bring it to the cross, and allow the blood of Christ to cleanse us from all unrighteousness.

While all wrongdoing is sin, not all sins are exactly the same. Thank God, however, that the cure for each one has already been discovered. It is salvation by faith in Christ alone.

*Heavenly Father, show us the particular sins
that affect our lives and marriage. We wish to
confess, renounce, and resist them. Amen.*

*Blessed is the one whose transgressions are forgiven,*
*whose sins are covered.*

PSALM 32:1

How may I forgive thee? Let me count the ways.

One of the most difficult challenges of marriage is to maintain a spirit of forgiveness. Our fallen human nature bristles at the idea of letting someone off the hook when they have wronged us. Yet the Bible tells us God delights in forgiving our sins in a variety of ways—ways that we experience each day. In Psalm 32 the word *forgiven* means God "carries away" our sin, removing both the guilt and the remembrance of sin. The word for *covered* refers to God's gracious decision to "never use our sin against us again" in the future. The expression *does not count* (v. 2) refers to God's declaration we are "not guilty."

So if God can find three ways to say He forgives us, can't we find at least one way to say it to our life partner today?

*Our forgiving God, please pardon us for being*
*so reluctant to offer others the forgiveness You*
*so freely offer us. Help us to live by the truth,*
*"Freely you have received, freely give,"*
*particularly in our marriage.*
*In Jesus' Name, Amen.*

*Therefore let all the faithful pray to you*
*while you may be found;*
*surely the rising of the mighty waters*
*will not reach them.*

Psalm 32:6

Do you have flood assurance?
No, we didn't mean to say flood insurance, but rather flood assurance. What in the world are we talking about?

The psalmist tells us flood assurance is the confidence we can receive ahead of time from God that should trouble deluge our home and marriage, He will protect and deliver us. This is true whether the inundation arrives from the outside world or whether it swirls up from within our lives. We can have the sweet assurance that life's deluges will not overwhelm us because of the unchanging promises of God's Word and His love that will keep us afloat.

So take heart, even when the waters rise, the sandbags of God's love and protection will always be twelve inches higher than the highest crest of the flood.

*Heavenly Father, thank You that You foresee*
*the raging water that will eventually enter our*
*lives long before it arrives. Help us to rest in*
*the assurance that however strong the rushing*
*torrents, You will keep us safe and dry in Your*
*loving arms. Amen.*

*Do not be like the horse or the mule,*
*which have no understanding*
*but must be controlled by bit and bridle*
*or they will not come to you.*

PSALM 32:9

Are you as stubborn as a mule?

There are two ways to get a mule to go the right direction. The first is simply to tell him to go to the right or to the left. If that doesn't work, then a good, strong jerk on a bit and bridle is the only option left. The Bible tells us we can sometimes act like mules when it comes to obeying the Lord. Is God telling us to spend more time in prayer together? Is He directing us to set aside family devotions in the Word of God each day? Is He prompting us to begin tithing to our church?

We can either respond to God's Spirit by acting in obedience at once or by digging in our heels, requiring stronger measures for God to get our cooperation. Both are prompted by God's love for us, but one is far easier to experience than the other.

*Dear God, allow us to come to You in humil-*
*ity and obedience at Your very first prompting*
*rather than foolishly resisting. Amen.*

*And we know that in all things God works
for the good of those who love him, who have
been called according to his purpose.*

ROMANS 8:28

Where is God when trouble enters our marriage? Perhaps it was easy to believe in the goodness of God the day we were married. The church was filled with flowers, friends wore elegant dresses and tuxedos, and seated before us was a sea of smiling well-wishers. Yet, as we all come to discover sooner or later, life is not an eternal wedding day. It becomes more difficult to believe in the goodness of God when our spouse contracts a dangerous disease, suffers a miscarriage, or admits they have a problem with Internet pornography. But the Scriptures teach God's good intentions toward our lives are always present. In all things He works for our good and His glory.

So where is God when trouble enters our marriage? Where He always is and shall always be—walking right beside us to accomplish His eternal and loving purposes.

*All-powerful God, help us to find the rest and
assurance we need that in all the circumstances we face today, we remain under Your
sovereign and loving care. Amen.*

*And I pray that you, being rooted and established*
*in love, may have power, together with all*
*the Lord's holy people, to grasp how wide and*
*long and high and deep is the love of Christ.*

EPHESIANS 3:17-18

Is love a renewable resource?

Huge iron ore deposits were discovered in Minnesota early in the nineteenth century. Fifty years later the Iron Range, as it is called, looked like a moonscape pocked with huge empty craters. Once the valuable ore was mined from the open pits, they were simply abandoned.

Many couples assume love is much like iron ore. There is only so much of it in the ground, and once the deposits are exhausted, it's gone for good. But Scripture teaches love is an infinitely renewable resource. As much as we might mine from the heart of God and give to one another, there is always an infinite amount still remaining.

Let's not be afraid to give away our love to our spouse and children; there's more of love where that came from—more than we can mine in a lifetime.

*Lord Jesus, thank You that Your love is*
*measureless and without end. May our*
*hearts be filled to overflowing all the*
*days of our life. Amen.*

*Therefore let us keep the Festival, not with the old
bread leavened with malice and wickedness, but
with the unleavened bread of sincerity and truth.*

1 Corinthians 5:8

Is angry humor all that funny?

We routinely receive e-mails that contain marriage humor, and much of it is tinged with anger and sarcasm. Anger is really sarcasm turned inside out and the resentment shows. Angry humor really is not funny because it gets a laugh at someone else's expense. While some stories may be admittedly clever, they are based on the notion that marriage is universally disappointing, constraining, and even hurtful to our lives.

Just the opposite is true. Marriage as God intended is to be a lifelong cause for joy, thanksgiving, and contentment. Let's avoid sarcastic humor in our marriage. It is only a front for an angry and disappointed heart, and there's nothing funny about that. Why not instead tell a story that builds up our spouse in front of others?

*Lord Jesus, if there is hidden anger or hurt in
our hearts toward one another, please rid us
of it before this day is over. Let our speech
consistently reflect the tender love and
respect we have for another. Amen.*

*Now there is in store for me the crown of righteousness,*
*which the Lord, the righteous Judge, will award*
*to me on that day—and not only to me, but*
*also to all who have longed for his appearing.*

2 Timothy 4:8

Are we willing to enjoy today but live for tomorrow? Most of life's sweetest rewards are ones we must wait for. When we first marry, we are usually short on money and long on dreams. Our first apartment is small, our first job is usually entry-level, and our first few years are marked by numerous adjustments. But we press on because we believe hard work and sacrifice will one day pay off and things will improve.

The same anticipation of future rewards should apply to our eternal home. In heaven we can anticipate receiving rewards from God Himself if we have kept our wedding vows, loved our spouse, and honored Christ with our resources. Regardless of how long we've been married, we should enjoy today, but should live for tomorrow. It will be a truly glorious day when our final reward arrives.

*O eternal God, allow us to live together in*
*such a way now that we shall one day hear,*
*"Well done, good and faithful spouse." Amen.*

*Many are the woes of the wicked,*
*but the LORD's unfailing love*
*surrounds the man who trusts in him.*

PSALM 32:10

What's the best security system for your home?
Companies make huge money these days
installing sophisticated security systems in private homes.
Through the miracle of technology, silent electronic sentries are stationed at windows or doors to detect the slightest movement or possibility of an intruder.

The Bible teaches that only one security system can
offer a home complete and absolute 24/7 security—it is
the Lord's unfailing love that surrounds the person who
trusts in Him. That means we can trust Him to stand
guard over our marriage, children, and our safety seven
days a week, twenty-four hours a day, caring for us and
those we love.

The only provision is that we must place our complete
confidence in His Name and Word. Once we do that, we
can sleep peacefully—He's got us surrounded.

*O Savior, thank You that we can live this life*
*without fear or anxiety of what may happen*
*to us. Help us to rest in the sweet truth and*
*assurance that Your love and power surround*
*us day and night. Amen.*

*For I am convinced that neither death nor life, neither*
*angels nor demons, neither the present nor the*
*future, nor any powers, neither height nor depth, nor*
*anything else in all creation, will be able to separate us*
*from the love of God that is in Christ Jesus our Lord.*

ROMANS 8:38-39

Can God lose you in a crowd?

Have you ever attended a major sporting event or concert with your children or another couple and found yourselves temporarily separated? One moment you were walking right next to each other, and the next they seem to have vanished. Usually it takes only a few moments to reconnect.

We are thankful that God never loses sight of us. The Bible teaches that when we commit our lives and marriage to Christ, we are forever joined to His presence and His love. Nothing in this life or the next, no power on earth or under the earth, can separate us from the love of God that is in Christ Jesus.

No need for a Lost and Found when Christ is our faithful life companion.

*Faithful Savior, help us to be ever aware in*
*our daily lives of Your presence, and to never*
*doubt that faithful companionship. Amen.*

*I will extol the Lord at all times;*
*his praise will always be on my lips.*
*I will glory in the Lord; let the afflicted hear*
*and rejoice. Glorify the Lord with me;*
*let us exalt his name together.*

Psalm 34:1-3

Whath's our best weapon against discouragement?
Discouragement can strike any marriage. When money runs low, tempers run high, and good news seems in short supply, it's easy to slide down into the long, dark tunnel of despondency.

So what's our best weapon in marriage against the quicksand of hopelessness?

The answer is to give God our praise. When things go terribly wrong, start praising Jesus immediately and we should not stop until we feel the burden of our spirits lifted. Praise is a powerful weapon that slays the dragons of defeat and despair. It changes our focus from earth to heaven, and soon even the worst circumstances lose their hold on our lives.

There's an old saying, "Praise God and pass the ammunition." Well, praising God is the ammunition to defeat all that would come against us.

*Lord Jesus, give us the faith to turn our*
*despairing emotions into expressions of praise,*
*believing You are always up to something good*
*in our lives. Amen.*

*Children's children are a crown to the aged,*
*and parents are the pride of their children.*

PROVERBS 17:6

Do you want your children to marry someone just like you?

All of us want the best future for our children. We want them to grow up to become well-adjusted persons, productive citizens, and happily married husbands or wives. But would that happen if they were to grow up and marry someone just like you?

It all depends on how we love and treat our spouse today. If we are modeling a life of love, patience, honor, fidelity, and respect toward our partner, chances are excellent our son or daughter will look for someone just like us. But if we are modeling a life of anger, cynicism, alienation, sarcasm, and disrespect—guess what? Chances are our son or daughter will marry someone just like us as well.

We consider the condition of our marriage today. It may well be the condition of our children's marriage tomorrow.

*Our precious Lord, create in us a bond of*
*unity and love that will be an example to our*
*children and grandchildren. Let them see the*
*living Christ clearly present in all our speech,*
*behavior, and attitudes. Amen.*

*Teach us to number our days,*
*that we may gain a heart of wisdom.*

PSALM 90:12

Is life what happens while we are preparing to live?

One of the most dangerous words to enter any marriage is *tomorrow*. Tomorrow I'll deal with my outbursts of anger. Tomorrow I'll start spending more time at home. Tomorrow I'll schedule a getaway with my spouse or sign up for that marriage enrichment weekend.

Unfortunately life is what happens to us while we are preparing to live. If we do not address the issues in our marriage today, the tomorrow we are planning may never arrive. We will find a week, then a month, then finally a year slipping away from us. We may wake up one day to realize that we have let an entire lifetime of opportunities go by.

We've talked with more than one regretful couple who wished they had never said, "Tomorrow." Today is the only day we have to invest in our marriage and make the needed changes. Don't let it slip away.

*Our loving God, keep us from putting off*
*till tomorrow what we should be doing right*
*now. Today, if we hear Your Spirit prompt-*
*ing us, may You keep us from hardening our*
*hearts. Amen.*

*All at once he followed her*
*like an ox going to the slaughter…*
*like a bird darting into a snare,*
*little knowing it will cost him his life.*

PROVERBS 7:22-23

Do you realize lures are just hooks dressed up to look good?

We love to go fishing in Canada. The bright blue sky, the sparkling lakes, and the abundant supply of fish make it a sportsman's dream. We use fluorescent artificial lures, small silver spoons intended to fool fish into thinking they are swallowing a minnow rather than a hook. But the lures turn out to be a noose, not a source of nourishment.

The same is true of sexual temptations in marriage. They present themselves as a way of nourishing our emotional and physical needs, but they trap us in a cruel net of humiliation, betrayal, and destruction. We are not to give sexual lures even a second glance as they pass by. Rather we must swim as fast as we can in the other direction until we are safely away.

Otherwise, we may one day find ourselves dangling from the devil's stringer of captured prey.

*Heavenly Father, lead us not into temptation,*
*but deliver us from the evil one. Amen.*

*Elijah went before the people and said, "How long
will you waver between two opinions? If the LORD
is God, follow him; but if Baal is God, follow him."
But the people said nothing.*

1 KINGS 18:21

Are you deciding whether to take the up or down escalator?

When we were children, we enjoyed riding escalators. Then as now there is always a choice that governs these miraculous moving staircases. We must choose whether to go up or whether to go down. We can't ride both at the same time.

The same is true in our marriage. Either our marriage is steadily growing, improving, and becoming more of what God intended, or it is stagnating, shriveling, and headed toward failure. It's time to quit wavering and step onto the up escalator. That may involve recommitting our lives to Christ, spending time in God's Word together, and living out our vows with a fresh vigor.

Once we step onto God's upward escalator, we are headed for the top floor of His will for our relationship. And please, watch your step.

*Lord Jesus, help us to quit wavering between
two opinions and make the choice to press
on toward our high and heavenly calling in
Christ Jesus. Amen.*

*What Jesus did here in Cana of Galilee was the first of the signs through which he revealed his glory; and his disciples believed in him.*

JOHN 2:11

Why did Jesus change water into wine?

The first recorded miracle of Jesus occurs at a wedding. He did not heal someone nor raise someone from the dead, but instead saved a young couple from humiliation. The custom of the day was to provide wine for the guests as long as the celebration continued. Yet, for reasons we are not told, the wine ran out before the reception did.

Jesus stepped in for three reasons: First, to demonstrate His love for the couple; second, to show His honor for the institution of marriage; and finally, to demonstrate He was the Son of God. Jesus is willing to reveal these same divine attributes in our marriages regardless of the problems we face.

Let's invite Him as the Guest of Honor into our marriage and watch the ordinary be transformed into the miraculous.

*Lord Jesus, we sometimes must face problems for which there seems to be no ready solution. Yet we know nothing is impossible with You. We invite Your presence into our dilemmas to reveal Your glory. Amen.*

*Nowhere in all the land were there found women as beautiful as Job's daughters, and their father granted them an inheritance along with their brothers.*

Job 42:15

Do we remember our wife was once daddy's little girl? Husbands, how well are we treating our wife? Here's a challenge for all men still raising young daughters at home. Can we imagine our little girl growing up to someday be ridiculed, ignored, or even demeaned by her future husband? Just the thought of that might well make us very upset. *How dare someone treat my little girl that way?*

Well, it's helpful for us to remember that our wives were once someone's little girl. If their fathers could see how we're treating them today, what would they think? Husbands, let's commit ourselves to remembering our wives deserve all the kindness, patience, and unconditional love we show to our young children—and more. The more we treat our wives as we should, the more likely our daughters will grow up to enjoy the same loving attitudes from their husbands.

*Heavenly Father, help us husbands to remember how precious our wives are. May we show them an even greater love and tenderness than they experienced as children in their father's home. Amen.*

*"They are like a man building a house, who dug down deep and laid the foundation on rock. When a flood came, the torrent struck that house but could not shake it, because it was well built."*

LUKE 6:48

Are we building a household of faith or fear?

In our married lives we have watched at least two homes we purchased be built from the ground up. We were there when they dug the hole, poured the foundation, framed out the rooms, added the insulation, and finally nailed down the roof. We observed firsthand the quality of the materials going into our future homes.

What about our household of relationships? Are we constructing it with materials that will last for all eternity? Or will our house collapse under a flood of worries, problems, and setbacks? We all are building a household of faith or a shack of fear. To build the former, we must place our complete faith in Christ and His work on the cross. He who was a carpenter knows how to build our home so that it endures now and for eternity.

*Lord Jesus, help us to hear Your words and put them into practice so that regardless of what comes our way, our home will stand. Amen.*

*"Therefore let all Israel be assured of
this: God has made this Jesus, whom you
crucified, both Lord and Messiah."*

Acts 2:36

Do we remember there's a throne over our home?
One of the great truths of the Christian faith is the simple proclamation "Jesus is Lord." That short but profound statement should encourage us. The Bible teaches that His throne rules over all the earth, including over our home and marriage.

Why is that encouraging news? It means there is no problem, worry, or troubling circumstance we face at this moment that isn't under the lordship of Jesus. That assures us that His all-powerful, all-wise, and all-loving character will safeguard all we commit to His care. The Holy Spirit can turn back all the forces of darkness and empower us to conquer whatever obstacles we encounter. Ultimately, we know His sovereign will shall be done on earth as it is in heaven.

Regardless of the problem we face at this moment, we should turn to each other and say with confidence, "Remember, Jesus is Lord over this."

*Our sovereign Lord, thank You that all of
heaven's power and authority is focused on our
daily lives as we exalt You as Savior and Lord.
Amen.*

*Since, then, you have been raised with*
*Christ, set your hearts on things above, where*
*Christ is, seated at the right hand of God.*

Colossians 3:1

Are we living a horizontal or a vertical life?

A horizontal life is oriented to this world and all it has to offer: money, prestige, power, and entertainment for its own sake. It is directed toward the here and now with seldom a thought of eternity. It is the way of the world.

A vertical life is oriented to God and His kingdom. It is constantly aware that this world is temporary and God's kingdom is forever. The focus is always on questions such as: What could we do to please God? What decisions will bring us closer to Jesus Christ? What opportunities do we have to share our faith with others?

Every couple has a choice to make—will we live a horizontal life that is temporary at best or a vertical life that will last forever? What's our angle?

*Lord Jesus, save us from living our lives on the*
*horizontal level. Train us to set our hearts on*
*things above, even as we go about our daily*
*duties and necessities. Amen.*

*"Very truly I tell you, whoever hears my word and
believes him who sent me has eternal life and will not
be judged but has crossed over from death to life."*

JOHN 5:24

How can we know whether we are living a temporary
or an eternal life?

Let's start with how we begin the day. When we
wake up, are we immediately wrestling with the worries,
demands, and problems of the day? Or do we open our
eyes and soon pray, *Lord, regardless of what we will face this
day, please let us live out Your joy and peace.*

The difference between these two perspectives will
affect how we respond to our spouse. If we are living a
temporary life and our spouse falls short of our expectations, we may choose to marginalize or withdraw from
them. But if we are living an eternal life and we are disappointed by our spouse, we will continue to love them, seek
their best, and by faith deliberately say no to our darkest
temptations to hurt them back.

*Precious Savior, in every area of our lives this
day, keep our focus on the eternal life that we
have received in You. Amen.*

*"But small is the gate and narrow the road
that leads to life, and only a few find it."*

MATTHEW 7:14

Wh    hat is the road less traveled?
         Call us foolish for enjoying getting off freeways
and driving two-lane roads instead. Sure the speed limit
is slower, and we have to go through one small town after
another. Yet how much more interesting and enjoyable
life can be when we take the road less traveled.

The same is true in our spiritual choices: we can either
live the life we want for ourselves or we can live the life
God has for us. One life we direct; the other life God
directs. One life is based on circumstances; the other life
is based on faith. One life accomplishes our goals; the
other God's eternal purposes for us. One life ends when
our time on earth comes to a conclusion; the other is eternal and has no terminal point. One life puts self on the
throne; the other seats Jesus Christ as Lord.

Which road will the two of you travel in your marriage? The choice will determine your ultimate destination.

*Dear Jesus, may we be among those You said
would find the road that leads to life. Amen.*

*"But because my servant Caleb has a different spirit and*
*follows me wholeheartedly, I will bring him into the*
*land he went to, and his descendants will inherit it."*

NUMBERS 14:24

Do we have Caleb-sized faith?

The Old Testament tells the fascinating story of a party of twelve spies who went out to survey the land God promised to the people of Israel. They all observed the same people, surveyed the same cities, and tasted of the same fruit. Yet when they returned to camp they gave wildly different accounts. Ten of the spies were absolutely panic-stricken at the size of the people and the thickness of the city walls, and they recommended a full retreat. Caleb and Joshua, however, were utterly confident of victory and urged the people to go forward full-speed to possess the land promised by God.

What about the two of us? Do we fixate on the size of our problems or on the size of the God we serve? God is looking for couples with Caleb-like faith to lay hold of all His promises.

*O powerful God, grant us a spirit like Caleb*
*and Joshua. By faith help us to see how*
*big You are and not the magnitude*
*of our problems. Amen.*

*Having been buried with him in baptism, in which*
*you were also raised with him through your faith in*
*the working of God, who raised him from the dead.*

COLOSSIANS 2:12

Do we remember God raises the dead?
One of the key truths of Scripture is that when we accept Jesus Christ as our Savior, we undergo a resurrection. He was raised from death to life, so now we walk out of the tomb of spiritual deadness into a wonderful new life based on faith in Christ. From that day onward, we live with the confidence that God raises the dead.

That resurrection can have an impact on every issue we face in this life. We may have regrets from our former life, but we know God raises the dead. We may have seen our dreams wither and die, but God raises the dead. We may have seen people taken from us that were so precious, but God raises the dead.

We can face all our problems each and every day with a resurrection outlook and discover the joy of what it means to be raised with Christ.

*Almighty God, thank You that in Christ we*
*have been raised from the dead and now*
*possess His resurrection power. Amen.*

*Sin is not ended by multiplying words,*
*but the prudent hold their tongues.*

Proverbs 10:19

Can we hold that thought?
Have we ever stumbled across a situation that irritated us? Perhaps the groceries were never put away the night before. Maybe we tripped over laundry that should have been put away yesterday. Or we discover a bill that was supposed to be mailed last week and is now overdue.

Our first instinct might be to find our spouse and point out their error. But what if we held that judgmental thought? What if instead we went into the kitchen and put away the fresh produce, stooped over and picked up the dirty socks on the floor, or simply paid the overdue bill online? What if instead of scolding our spouse we served them instead? It might spare our partner and our children an unnecessary ugly moment.

There are times we need to hold that thought. It may give us time to remember relationships are the most important aspect of a family and preserving them is all important.

*Heavenly Father, the tongue is a difficult*
*creature to tame. Grant us the wisdom to*
*hold our thoughts until we have carefully*
*considered their long-term impact. Amen.*

*"In your anger do not sin": Do not let the
sun go down while you are still angry, and
do not give the devil a foothold.*

EPHESIANS 4:26-27

Can we make the "quick adjustment"?

How long does it take us to forgive our spouse
when they ask us to? For some people, they have to brood
for the rest of the morning. For others it even drags on
to the next day. Unfortunately for others, grievances are
carried for years and decades. The longer we brood, the
greater the damage to our marriage.

One devotional writer gave this immensely practical
advice: "Make the quick adjustment." We should choose
not only to forgive our spouse, but choose to soon adjust
our emotions toward them as well. Go back to treating
them with courtesy, warmth, and intimacy as soon as possible.

The Bible reflects this same wisdom when we are told
not to let "the sun go down while [we] are still angry." The
quick adjustment is one more way to ensure our love is
long-lasting.

*Lord Jesus, let Your love and peace rather than
anger and resentment rule our hearts. Help us
to quickly return to a state of love whenever it
is disrupted. Amen.*

*Children are a heritage from the LORD,*
*offspring a reward from him.*

PSALM 127:3

What do most men in their fifties regret?

Patrick Morley wrote a widely acclaimed book for men titled *Man in the Mirror*. In his chapter on raising children with no regrets, he remarks that in a survey of men in their fifties, one of their main sorrows was how little time they spent with their children. Often those early years are spent building a career, earning an income, and planning for retirement. By the time our children reach adolescence, their desire to spend time with us is replaced by a desire to be with peers. By then we may have already lost 80 percent of our opportunity to spend large quantities of time with our kids.

The challenge is to make the most of the hours we've been given with our children. All too soon we will be taking their senior picture and sending them off to their future. As parents we need to intentionally involve ourselves today so that we won't regret our choices tomorrow.

*Our Lord Jesus, today is the day to love our*
*children and engage them in our lives. Help us*
*to pass on all other fleeting priorities. Amen.*

*For you know that we dealt with each of you as a*
*father deals with his own children, encouraging,*
*comforting and urging you to live lives worthy of*
*God, who calls you into his kingdom and glory.*

1 Thessalonians 2:11-12

Is today a day wasted or a life forever changed?

It is said that Charles Francis Scott, a nineteenth-century diplomat, recorded in his diary the following entry: "Went fishing with my son today—a day wasted." His son, Brook, also kept a diary. That same day his son wrote, "Went fishing with my father—the most wonderful day of my life!"

Fathers, we must never forget that what may seem like a waste of time to us may be the day that changes the life of our son or daughter. The time we spend together will be forever recorded, not only in their memory but also in their heart. A day invested in our children is never a waste, but one that will influence generations to come.

*Heavenly Father, give us eyes to see life through*
*the eyes of our children. Allow us to know how*
*precious time spent together is to their hearts*
*and minds. Amen.*

*Therefore, if anyone is in Christ, the new creation
has come: The old has gone, the new is here!*

2 Corinthians 5:17

Can we please identify ourselves?

Secular recovery groups have become quite popular in our culture. One of our concerns is that often such groups insist that we identify ourselves according to our addiction or problem. "I am a recovering alcoholic (or overeater, or drug user, or…)." They further insist we keep this recovery addiction-identity the rest of our life. It is part of staying honest and away from denial.

According to the Bible, that approach is not entirely correct. The Scriptures tell us that if we are in Christ, we are a new creation. The old has gone, and the new has come. The right answer to the question of our identity is now, "I am a child of God, a new creation of Jesus Christ, who happens to struggle with this particular issue."

What Christ has done for us, not our struggle, defines us. A new identity gives us power to lead a new life.

*O victorious Savior, thank You for giving us a
new identity based on Your finished work on
the cross. May we daily claim the power and
freedom that victory offers. Amen.*

*For the Lord himself will come down from
heaven, with a loud command, with the voice
of the archangel and with the trumpet call of
God, and the dead in Christ will rise first.*

1 Thessalonians 4:16

Do we live with a Second Coming certainty?
It's common to experience anxiety over the problems we face. Perhaps our daughter needs expensive braces or there are rumors at work of impending layoffs or we received a troubling medical report. One way to address such worries is to take the long view. Ask the question, "Even if the worst thing we could imagine happens to us, what happens after that?" If we keep pursuing that line of questioning, we should eventually arrive at this comforting answer: "Then Christ will return for us."

Despite how grim or depressing today's issues may be, remember this comforting truth: "And after this, Christ will return for us." A Second Coming certainty offers us just the hope we need to victoriously overcome whatever worry we face today.

*O coming Savior, remind us daily that
the problem we confront is not the end of the
world. Only Your return is the end of
the world, and that will be a truly
glorious finish. Amen.*

*Finally, be strong in the Lord and in his mighty power. Put on the full armor of God, so that you can take your stand against the devil's schemes.*

EPHESIANS 6:10-11

D id we dress in spiritual armor today?

Many Christians mistakenly believe that if they don't mention the devil, he will forget about them and leave them alone. Unfortunately, nothing could be further from the truth. The Bible tells us we face an adversary who prowls around looking for someone to devour (1 Peter 5:8). So the only true protection a Christian marriage or home can have from the ravenous beast is to put on the full armor of God each day.

How do we do that? We pray together that God will equip us with His helmet of salvation, the breastplate of righteousness, the belt of truth, the sandals of gospel peace, the shield of faith, and the sword of the Spirit, which is God's Word. We don't dress only for success each day; we dress for the duress that could come our way. That requires the whole armor of God.

*Dear Lord, we are in a spiritual war whether we wish to be or not. Help us to be strong in You and in Your mighty power. Amen.*

*"Honor your father and your mother, so that you may
live long in the land the LORD your God is giving you."*

EXODUS 20:12

Can our children help us know how we are treating
our spouse?

Husbands and wives, here's a simple test to find out
how much love and respect we are showing toward each
other. Let's stop and listen to how our children talk to
our spouse (or about them). They are often an amazingly
accurate mirror of our own behavior. If we consistently
show our spouse love and respect, we will find our children following our lead. However, if we consistently criticize or demean our partner, we shouldn't be surprised
when we see our children doing exactly the same thing.
They learned it from Dad and Mom. Whatever we want to
hear from our children, they must hear from our lips first.

The Ten Commandments teach that children are to
show honor to their father and mother—that honor starts
with the two of us. As the old saying goes, "The apple
never falls too far from the tree."

*Lord Jesus, our spouse deserves our highest love
and respect. Help us to model that dignifying
and godly behavior before our children so they
will in turn do the same. Amen.*

*In the time of Herod king of Judea there was a priest named Zechariah...his wife Elizabeth was also a descendant of Aaron...But they were childless because Elizabeth was not able to conceive, and they were both very old.*

LUKE 1:5,7

Is the nest ever empty if we have each other?

We once visited an elderly couple in the hospital where the husband was recovering from surgery. We asked them how it felt to be alone now their children were grown up and gone. They both looked at us and smiled. "Why, we're not alone. We have each other."

In that moment we realized all over again the wonderful plan God has created for marriage in our lives. Parents may age and die. Children may grow up and leave home. Friends may move away. But as long as we still have each other, we will never be alone.

So don't fear the future. God gave us to one another to face each coming day together. We should pour ourselves into the one relationship that is intended to go the entire distance of life.

*Heavenly Father, thank You for creating our marriage to last a lifetime. May we walk this life's journey hand in hand. Amen.*

*My dear brothers and sisters, take note of
this: Everyone should be quick to listen.*

JAMES 1:19

I heard what you said, but did I hear what you meant?

There's a well-traveled story about a husband who asked his wife what she would like for her birthday. "I'd like to be six again," she said with a wistful look in her eye. Immediately the husband began planning her special day. When her birthday arrived, he first took her to an amusement park for four hours of nonstop roller-coaster rides. Later he drove her to an ice cream shop and insisted she order the largest banana split they could make. He finished the day off with a picnic and two hours at a playground. At the end of the day he asked her proudly, "Well, how did you enjoy your birthday?"

"I hated it," she said. "I'm tired, dizzy, and sick to my stomach."

"I thought you wanted to be six again."

"I meant *size* six," she replied.

Husbands, we may hear what she said, but did we hear what she meant?

*Dear Lord, may we desire more to hear than
to be heard, more to understand than to be
understood, and even more to love than to be
loved. Amen.*

*However, each one of you also must love his wife as he*
*loves himself, and the wife must respect her husband.*

Ephesians 5:33

Are we our spouse's keeper?

The apostle Paul tells husbands and wives they have a unique and lifelong obligation toward one another. "Husbands, love your wives," he simply states. For our entire lives we are commanded not only to show love toward our spouse, but to protect and guard her from those who would mistreat her as well. We are our wife's keeper.

Then Paul simply says, "Respect your husbands." That implies not only a lifelong obligation to show honor and admiration to our husband, but to insist that our children, parents, and other relatives do as well. When others would devalue or insult his place of leadership, wives are to step in and say, "No, that's not right." In short, we are to be our husband's keeper.

We are to be each other's first line of defense in a world that is often hostile and uncaring. The result is a marriage and home that prospers in season and out of season.

*Our blessed Savior, remind us continually of*
*the vows we made to keep one another the day*
*we married. Amen.*

*I will not look with approval*
*on anything that is vile.*

PSALM 101:3

D o we have the courage to change the channel?
Television and the Internet are rife with images
and situations meant to arouse and tease the viewer's
imagination—particularly for men. But do we realize
that such soft-core pornography exacts a high price on
marriages? More than one clinical study has demonstrated
that men who view pornography experience less satisfaction with their marriage and place a lower value on marriage. Isn't that a terribly huge price to pay for watching
racy situation comedies on high-definition television or
provocative movies on your laptop?

Husbands, let's take a radical step today to preserve
the sanctity and satisfaction of our marriage. Get up and
change the channel or close that site immediately whenever objectionable programming or images appear. Such
decisive action will speak volumes to our spouse (and to
our children) that we are determined to protect and value
our marriage.

*Lord Jesus, You have said that to look upon a*
*woman with lust is to commit adultery in our*
*heart. Keep us from such willful sins and let*
*no vile thing be set before our eyes. Amen.*

*The acts of the flesh are obvious…hatred, discord,*
*jealousy, fits of rage, selfish ambition, dissensions,*
*factions and envy; drunkenness, orgies, and the like.*

GALATIANS 5:19-21

What can we build on a landfill?

A giant landfill in our city has reached its capacity. Local officials have covered it with grass, a few trees, and even located a par three golf course on its summit. But the problem remains—underneath it's still a garbage heap.

What can we build on top of a landfill? The answer is not much. The toxic groundwater, chemical contaminants, and methane gases will remain for decades or even centuries.

As married couples we would do well to consider that image. If we build our marriages on strife, anger, rage, malice, and unforgiveness, as the years go by a poisonous mound will grow. And in the end, we will be unable to build anything of value because the ground beneath is too poisoned. That's why it's vital we build our relationship daily on forgiveness, acceptance, and honor. You can construct a growing mountain of love on such wonderful elements.

*Lord Jesus, let love, joy, peace, patience, and*
*kindness be the foundation we build our*
*marriage upon. Amen.*

*Husbands, in the same way be considerate as you*
*live with your wives, and treat them with respect.*

1 PETER 3:7

D o we forget who will be driving us someday?
Every once in a while my dear wife helps me with
a much needed attitude adjustment. If I am momentarily
critical or inconsiderate, she will sweetly say, "Remember,
dear, I'll be the one driving you around someday."

She's probably right. Given decades of time and aging,
she will likely be the one with the health and vigor I will
then lack. I will have to depend on her to take me where I
need to go and to care for the things I can no longer care
for myself. It's a humbling thought, but one I need to
remember. When that day arrives, how will I want her to
treat me? Will I want scorn, correction, and scolding, or
mercy, patience, and respect?

The Bible tells husbands we are to show our wives con-
sideration and respect throughout our lives together. Husbands, let's be careful how we treat our wife today. She may
be driving us around tomorrow.

*Heavenly Father, may we treat each other*
*exactly the way we would want to be treated.*
*Amen.*

*May the L*ORD *bless you from Zion;*
*may you see the prosperity of Jerusalem*
*all the days of your life. May you live*
*to see your children's children.*

PSALM 128:5-6

Should we act more like grandparents toward our children?

We read a comedian who said, "When I would ask my dad for fifty cents growing up, he would tell me how hard he had to work and how far he had to walk to school and then say no. Now that he's a grandfather, he hands out ten and twenty dollar bills to my children when they just walk through the room."

While there's obvious overstatement involved, the point is worth remembering. Wise grandparents typically treat their grandchildren with unusual amounts of love, tenderness, value, and patience. They've learned how short life is and how precious relationships are. Why don't we begin acting a little more like a grandparent today while our children are still children? We should not overindulge or spoil them, but perhaps relax and open up our heart more.

It's never too soon for us to start acting like a loving grandparent.

*Dear Lord, may we shower our children today*
*with all the loving traits we will one day freely*
*give to their children. Amen.*

*"But if you do not forgive others their sins,*
*your Father will not forgive your sins."*

MATTHEW 6:15

Is our world shrinking or expanding?

There is a high and hidden cost to unforgiveness in a marriage. When we refuse to forgive our husband or wife despite a sincere and heartfelt apology, our world shrinks just a few inches. We no longer enjoy with our spouse the same width and breadth and length of joy, freedom, and intimacy we once did. Over time, our unforgiveness not only reduces our world but confines us in ever-narrowing circles of anger, distance, and bitterness.

Thankfully, by the grace of God, when we forgive our spouse (and others) from our hearts, just the opposite occurs. Our sphere of love, joy, and acceptance expands until we enjoy a breadth and quality of life hard to imagine. When we walk in freedom and harmony with others, forgiving quickly and accepting apologies, it opens up the way for God to do the same with us.

Let's not shrink our world or our marriage—let's forgive as Jesus Christ has forgiven us.

*Precious Savior, You freely and abundantly*
*forgive us our trespasses. Help us to be ready to*
*do the same to others. Amen.*

*See to it that no one falls short of the grace
of God and that no bitter root grows up
to cause trouble and defile many.*

HEBREWS 12:15

Do we know the true price of holding a grudge?
Have we ever stopped to consider the real hidden
costs of nursing resentment against our spouse? We're not
referring to extreme situations, such as adultery or severe
abuse, that require an in-depth process of forgiveness, reconciliation, and setting boundaries. We're referring to the
temptation to hold a grudge against our husband or wife
for their everyday annoying, disappointing, even infuriat-
ing habits or mistakes.

The true price of prideful unforgiveness includes
expending an enormous amount of emotional energy to
stay angry, disrupting the normal rhythms of married life,
becoming physically sick, and turning our home into a
place of tension and fear.

With such a high cost for holding a grudge, doesn't it
make sense to heed the Bible's simple advice to not miss
the grace of God and allow no bitter root to grow up?

*Forgiving God, we ask that no weed of resent-
ment ever take hold in our relationship. Let
us extend grace to one another as soon as it's
needed. Amen.*

*Bear with each other and forgive one another if
any of you has a grievance against someone.*

Colossians 3:13

Are there times when we are unbearable?

The Bible commands us to do something very difficult. It tells us to "bear with each other." How much easier it would be if Paul had just written "put up with each other" or "humor each other." We are called to do far more than that. The scriptural word is to patiently endure the shortcomings and imperfections of our spouse without reacting in anger or unkindness.

"Bearing with" is far more than just gritting our teeth and keeping our tongue when we want to lash out. It is lovingly looking beyond our spouse's faults and seeing their need. We may find our spouse too talkative, too quiet, too fat, too skinny, or a hundred other annoyances. The secret to lifelong love is to patiently endure and to love them for the gift they are.

Bearing with your spouse is a Christlike virtue we all can practice.

*Lord Jesus, how many times You have had to
bear with us in our weaknesses and sin. Give
us the will and the strength to do the same
with others, particularly those closest to us.
Amen.*

*Be kind and compassionate to one another, forgiving
each other, just as in Christ God forgave you.*

EPHESIANS 4:32

C an we pardon others as a way of life?
Presidential clemency often creates quite a stir in
the media. It's customary for presidents as they are leaving office to sign eleventh-hour pardons for convicted
criminals or those facing indictment. The law requires no
justification for their decisions nor can any court over-
turn these acts of pardon. The president sets someone free
simply out of mercy.

Such a decree of unmerited grace is the concept
behind the word *forgive* as it is found in the New Testament. We are to freely pardon our guilty brother or sister
because in Christ God has freely pardoned us.

Only a husband or wife has the power to release the
other spouse from their prison of guilt and spiritual debt.
They alone can sign the decree. But the good news is that
when we initial the pardon for our spouse, we both end
up going free.

> *Dear Friend Jesus, where would we be if You
> had not signed our pardon? Now give us the
> daily grace to freely offer each other what we
> have freely received—unconditional love and
> forgiveness. Amen.*

*[Love] does not dishonor others, it is not self-seeking,*
*it is not easily angered, it keeps no record of wrongs.*

1 Corinthians 13:5

Do we store grievances only to chew on them later?
In Bob's home state, the university's team mascot is a rather unlikely creature—a gopher. We've always wondered why they didn't choose something a bit more intimidating like a wildcat or dashing like a buccaneer or at least as swift as a panther. The most notable feature of gophers is their apparent ability to store acorns in their cheeks—only to chew on them at a later time.

Some marriages have chosen the gopher as their team mascot without knowing it. The offended mate stores grievances in their heart only to gnaw on them later over and over. They choose to carry resentments on indefinitely. That's the opposite practice of true biblical forgiveness. God's grace cancels our right to use our spouse's sin against them in the future. Godly love keeps no record of wrongs.

*Lord Jesus, we give You today the record of*
*wrongs we have kept and ask You to nail*
*them to the cross where You cancelled even the*
*remembrance of our own sins. Amen.*

*And over all these virtues put on love, which*
*binds them all together in perfect unity.*

Colossians 3:14

W hat is the glue of our marriage relationship?
While well-crafted puns may cause a groan, they often contain an element of truth. For example, did you hear about the semitruck that ran into an empty tollgate booth? The collision demolished the booth into dozens of pieces. Fortunately, alert tollway crews were able to quickly piece the structure back together using a white, creamy substance squeezed from a tube. What was this miracle glue? None other than tollgate booth paste.

Which raises the question, what is the glue of our marriage? Money? Physical attraction? Shared goals? The apostle Paul offers us the most powerful epoxy of all time: "And over all these virtues put on love, which binds them all together in perfect unity." Such Christlike love holds a marriage together through job layoffs, extended sickness, or prodigal children. It glues us to one another when the problems of life might tear apart our unity. It produces oneness that life cannot rend in two.

*Heavenly Father, we choose today to put on*
*the divine love that comes directly from Your*
*heart and binds us together for life. Amen.*

*The Lord has anointed me*
*to proclaim good news to the poor.*
*He has sent me to bind up the brokenhearted.*

Isaiah 61:1

H as life broken your heart?
Every so often we meet individuals who seem crushed by daily life. Perhaps they have been rejected by their husband or wife. Perhaps their parents never showed them love as a child. Perhaps a traumatic event left them scarred for a lifetime. What hope is there for such wounded souls?

Listen to the words of the beautiful hymn "Rescue the Perishing" written by Fanny Crosby in 1870: "Down in the human heart, crushed by the tempter, feelings lie buried that grace can restore; touched by a loving heart, wakened by kindness, chords that were broken will vibrate once more." The healing grace of the Lord Jesus, the kindness of God our Savior, can cause chords that life has broken to sing once more.

Let's turn to the Lord Jesus and allow Him to heal our heart. Let the music begin.

*Lord Jesus, thank You that You are the friend*
*of a broken heart. Speak Your Word to our*
*damaged hearts and restore them to a child-*
*like peace and trust. Touch our hearts just now.*
*Amen.*

*Then we will no longer be infants…Instead,*
*speaking the truth in love, we will grow to*
*become in every respect the mature body of*
*him who is the head, that is, Christ.*

EPHESIANS 4:14-15

How old are we?

We came across an electronic greeting card of a tough-looking cowboy in his late sixties. The caption read, "Aging is inevitable." The picture enlarged to show the rugged cowboy sitting on a mechanical horse outside a department store. These words appeared underneath: "But maturity is optional."

Yes, aging is inevitable, but growing up is optional. The goal of the Christian life is to "grow up" into Christ who is the head. Infanthood is characterized by instability, lack of consistency, and the tendency to be easily deceived. Maturity, however, brings stability, steadiness, and a certainty of the truth.

Perhaps we should measure our lives not in chronological years but in our growth in character and faith. That, according to the Scriptures, is what it means to be a true grown-up.

So let's tell the truth—how old are we?

*Our precious Savior, help us to put childish*
*ways behind us and to become fully mature in*
*You. Amen.*

*A gentle answer turns away wrath,*
*but a harsh word stirs up anger.*

PROVERBS 15:1

I s it a good idea to raise your voice?

We once read the story of neighbors who called the police to investigate loud noises coming from the apartment next door. When the authorities arrived, they found a seventy-six-year-old woman practicing for her yodeling diploma. The police filed the following statement: "The officers weren't able to judge whether the neighbors were unfamiliar with Bavarian folk music or whether the lady still requires a lot of practice."

Perhaps the real lesson of the story is this—it's never a good idea to raise your voice at home. When we show our irritation or anger through increased volume or emotional intensity, we are most often heading into unproductive and dangerous territory. It causes hurt in the heart of our spouse and pain in the lives of our children.

The Bible reminds us that a gentle answer turns away wrath. The next time we're tempted to turn up our voice at our spouse, we should remember that other people are listening—particularly our heavenly Father.

*Lord Jesus, teach us the virtue of gentleness*
*in all our conversations, especially those that*
*occur in our home each day. Amen.*

*"Blessed are the poor in spirit,
for theirs is the kingdom of heaven."*

MATTHEW 5:3

Remember when we had nothing but each other? We started our married life with little more than enough to fill half of the smallest trailer we could rent. Years later, though we were still living by modest standards, we needed half of a semitrailer to move our then family of eight from one city to another. Yet, as we look back at the days when we had little else but each other, we were more than satisfied.

God wants us to live our lives where He is more than enough. Jesus said the truly blessed are the poor in spirit, for they will receive the kingdom of heaven. When we are satisfied with God alone, we have come to possess true spiritual riches. While God may bless us with material things, once we are content with Him, there isn't a moving van in the entire world that can store the priceless treasures that are now ours.

*Dear God, grant us the wisdom to see that if
we have Jesus, we have all that we need. Let us
seek Your kingdom first and last. Amen.*

*"Where have you laid him?" [Jesus] asked.*
*"Come and see, Lord," they replied.*
*Jesus wept.*
*Then the Jews said, "See how he loved him!"*

JOHN 11:34-36

Are we aware that to grieve deeply is to have loved deeply?

From time to time we have the privilege of ministering to a recent widow or widower. Quite often they are struggling with how much they miss their spouse. Some will even apologize for displaying their overwhelming grief.

"Please don't apologize," we reply. "To grieve deeply means that you loved the person deeply. A far greater tragedy would be for you to feel nothing at all—that would mean there was little or no love in your relationship."

Yes, the day is coming where one of us will lose the other to age, disease, and ultimately death. But let us not fear the grief of that hour. Grief is simply the signature at the bottom of a lifelong love letter that confirms you two had something very special.

Love one another deeply today. It will remain beyond death.

*Resurrected Savior, You wept at the grave of*
*Lazarus because of Your great love. Give us*
*the freedom to do the same for those we have*
*loved so much. Amen.*

*Let the peace of Christ rule in your hearts, since as
members of one body you were called to peace.*

Colossians 3:15

Who is the referee in our home?

The New Testament throws down a bold challenge for a married couple: "Let the peace of Christ rule in your hearts." The word for *rule* is used only once in the entire New Testament. It is taken from the athletic games in the ancient world and describes those who would oversee the games. We might translate it in our culture as "referee" or "umpire."

The peace of Christ's Presence is to be the final referee or ultimate authority in our households. We are to let His Spirit umpire our discussions, finances, sexual relationship, disagreements, dreams, and the list goes on and on.

Our sinful human nature typically wants to rule the game and its outcome. Before we get into a power play with our spouse, let's step back and let the peace of Christ rule our hearts and words.

> *Lord and Master, we invite You to rule every
> aspect of our marriage and home. Let Your
> will in our lives be the final word. Amen.*

*Then Paul left the synagogue and went next door*
*to the house of Titius Justus, a worshiper of God.*

ACTS 18:7

Do we worship only on Sunday?

One of the most important aspects of our marriage is taking time to worship God together. Yet it is often one of the least noticed and most neglected aspects of our marriage. Our busy lives and frantic schedules can crowd out worship during the week.

If we worship together only on Sunday but neglect Monday through Saturday, we have marginalized God's Presence. In His place we foolishly substitute late-night television, countless hours spent on the Internet, and chasing entertainment in one form or another. Why not set aside time each day solely for the purpose of worship? It doesn't require a full worship team or a lengthy sermon, only stopping long enough to engage God's Word and call on His name in prayer.

Thankfully, we can make every day a day of worship in our home.

*Almighty God, forgive us for neglecting*
*worship in favor of lesser things. May we*
*worship You in Spirit and truth each day*
*of our lives. Amen.*

*"For where two or three gather in my
name, there am I with them."*

Matthew 18:20

Do we need a preacher, music, and offering to worship God?

One explanation why many, perhaps most, couples neglect the daily worship of God is a wrong concept of worship. We can mistakenly believe it occurs only in a church, complete with a praise band or choir, projection screen or hymnals, and a room full of people.

Scripture teaches the worship of God is available whenever two or more people gather in the name of Jesus to ascribe Him worth (from the Old English word *worth-ship*). Worship is essentially an attitude of the heart that does not require formal liturgies, expository preaching, or a missions offering (though all are elements of worship). What is vital to worship is to exalt the glorious name of Jesus together.

Even if it is just a congregation of the two of us, our living room can become a cathedral of praise and worship.

*Lord Jesus, make our home a place where we
attribute worth to You each and every day.
May Your Name be frequently on our lips and
constantly in our hearts. Amen.*

*Therefore, I urge you, brothers and sisters, in
view of God's mercy, to offer your bodies as a
living sacrifice, holy and pleasing to God—
this is your true and proper worship.*

ROMANS 12:1

Are we willing to sign terms of surrender?

Normally we think of surrender as a humiliating moment in life. It is the admission of defeat. It is the capitulation of our forces to superior forces. It typically spells the end of our freedoms.

But Scripture paints a very different picture of surrender. When Scripture tells us "to offer [our] bodies as a living sacrifice," this is not humiliation but victory. It is not defeat but worship. It is not the end of our freedoms but the route to a victorious, holy, and pleasing relationship with God. It is giving Christ His rightful rule over our life and will.

When we surrender our marriage to God, with all its problems and potential, Christ is able to bless it and nurture it and strengthen it in a way that pleases Him supremely. In spiritual terms, surrender is for winners, not losers. So where do we sign?

*Lord Jesus, we gladly surrender this day our
lives, marriage, and future to Your holy and
sovereign will. Amen.*

*"I pray…that all of them may be one, Father, just as
you are in me and I am in you. May they also be in us
so that the world may believe that you have sent me."*

John 17:21

Is the Trinity our model for marriage?

It may go without saying, but the Father, Son, and
Holy Spirit have never had an argument, a disagreement,
or a heated discussion. There has always been, always is,
and always will be perfect agreement, harmony, and unity.
As our passage today reveals, Jesus actually prayed that this
same supernatural unity might prevail among believers,
and that includes married believers.

So when we are at loggerheads over difficult issues, we
should stop and pray for God to grant us the same oneness
that exists among the Father, Son, and Holy Spirit. Can
we think of better role models for harmony in matrimony
than the Holy Trinity?

> *Father, Son, and Holy Spirit, grant us in all
> our day-to-day relationships the same love,
> fellowship, and unity that You have enjoyed
> throughout eternity. Amen.*

*"Your fasting ends in quarreling and strife,*
*and in striking each other with wicked fists.*
*You cannot fast as you do today*
*and expect your voice to be heard on high."*

ISAIAH 58:4

Is God turning a deaf ear to our prayers?

There are many reasons why prayers may go unanswered in a marriage. We may be asking with the wrong motives such as pride, selfishness, or foolishness. All these reasons and more can turn the heavens to brass.

But there may be another cause—one that we may have not considered—fighting between the two of us. The prophet Isaiah warns us that quarreling and strife can damage the impact of our fasting and prayer. You cannot act like you do today and expect your voice to be heard on high, he pronounces.

The spirit of discord and argument is offensive to God and creates barriers. For God to answer our prayers, we need to stop verbal sparring and instead lift holy hands toward heaven in humility and repentance. The willingness of heaven to hear and respond will suddenly change.

*Lord Jesus, remove any spirit of contention or*
*strife from our lives. Let us treat one another*
*with gentleness, civility, and kindness. Amen.*

*Rejoice always, pray continually, give
thanks in all circumstances; for this is
God's will for you in Christ Jesus.*

1 THESSALONIANS 5:16-18

Do we know the five game-changing words?
The Bible tells us there are five simple words that
can transform a miserable, lonely, and angry home into
one filled with contentment, meaningful relationships,
and an ongoing feast of joy. What are these remarkable
words? "Give thanks in all circumstances." It's that simple.

When we start each day by together giving thanks for
God's character, the generosity of His heart, and the wisdom of His choices over our lives, it begins to transform
our environment. When we give thanks for the person
we married, the children we've been given, and the family that's ours, it reshapes our perspective. Giving thanks
releases God's joy, blessing, and viewpoint on the problems facing us. It defeats the devil's plans to discourage
and depress us. We find ourselves rising above our every
circumstance with true joy, and we discover we are more
than conquerors in Jesus Christ.

Giving thanks is the ultimate game-changer.

*Merciful God, how can we begin to thank You
for all that You have done for us? Thank You
for the ultimate gift of Jesus Christ as the
Savior of the world. Amen.*

*And the words of the LORD are flawless,*
*like silver purified in a crucible,*
*like gold refined seven times.*

PSALM 12:6

Is the Bible simply intriguing or is it inerrant?

How we view the Bible will determine a great deal of our future. If we view it as merely interesting, we will likely leave it on a bookshelf, nightstand, or in the drawer. We will make our life decisions based only on what we think is best for us or to our advantage. Sadly, the end result will be more disappointments and heartaches than we can imagine. Why? Because human wisdom is simply that— it's human. It is therefore limited, circumscribed and corrupted with the weaknesses of a fallen world.

But if we view the Bible as God's Word, without error and the supreme authority over our life, our future will turn out quite differently. We will find God's wisdom, leadership, and guidance directing us day after day, year after year toward a wonderful end.

Is the Bible merely intriguing or is it without error? If there is dust on the cover, we should reconsider our answer.

*Lord Jesus, thank You that all Scripture is*
*flawless, more pure and precious than gold*
*refined seven times. Amen.*

*Through Jesus, therefore, let us continually
offer to God a sacrifice of praise—the fruit
of lips that openly profess his name.*

Hebrews 13:15

Do we regularly present the sacrifice of praise?

When we watch Olympic weightlifters hoist barbells the size of railroad car wheels above their head, it's clear they didn't start out that way. No doubt they began their careers by using lighter weights. As their strength increased and their muscles enlarged, they added heavier and heavier weights. Eventually the day came when they were ready for international competition.

It's much the same way in the Christian life. As we encounter the smaller difficulties of life and respond by offering God the sacrifice of praise, and we find His strength growing within, it prepares us to face more challenging obstacles. Eventually, we are prepared to face any and every obstacle life can throw at us by offering God praise.

Today let's praise Him for His loving character, sacrificial death, gift of eternal life, and soon return. Such faith-building worship will one day earn us heaven's gold medal, or as the Bible puts it, the crown of righteousness.

*Lord Jesus, as we experience life's hardships,
build our faith as we continually offer the
sacrifice of praise day after day. Amen.*

*And the twenty-four elders, who were seated
on their thrones before God, fell on their
faces and worshiped God, saying:
"We give thanks to you, Lord God Almighty,
the One who is and who was,
because you have taken your great power
and have begun to reign."*

REVELATION 11:16-17

Can a little heaven on earth come to our home?
Do we ever wonder what is happening in heaven
this very moment? What if we could pull back the curtain
of the spiritual universe and glimpse into the very throne
room of God? What would we see going on?

The Book of Revelation offers us one such quick
glimpse: in heaven at this very moment the hosts of glory
are giving thanks and praise. They are exalting God for
His eternal nature and for His sovereign rule over the
earth. What can we do to bring some of heaven into our
kitchen or driveway or backyard right now? Give thanks
to God and to Jesus Christ who reigns over all the earth
and sits in authority over our lives. It will be a tantalizing
taste of things to come.

*Coming King Jesus, we want to get a head
start on heaven. Thank You for who You are,
and reign over our home today. Amen.*

*"Our Father in heaven, hallowed be your name,*
*your kingdom come, your will be done, on*
*earth as it is in heaven. Give us today our daily*
*bread. And forgive us our debts, as we also*
*have forgiven our debtors. And lead us not into*
*temptation, but deliver us from the evil one."*

MATTHEW 6:9-13

How can the Lord's Prayer protect our marriage?
Do we sometimes find it difficult to pray with our spouse? Maybe the words come awkwardly, slowly, or not at all. Here's a simple suggestion that could turn things around: begin each day by praying the Lord's Prayer together. Tell God He is our Father and we desire to do His will. Ask Him to provide our family with our daily bread. Confess that we are willing to forgive each other in order to be forgiven. Implore God to keep us away from all temptation and to deliver us from the evil one. Let this prayer become a close and personal conversation with our heavenly Father from the deepest parts of our hearts.

If prayed in this spirit, God will use it to protect us and our marriage.

*Our Father, may we pray as the Lord Jesus*
*taught us to pray. Amen.*

*Let perseverance finish its work so that you may be mature and complete, not lacking anything.*

JAMES 1:4

Is crisis an opportunity in disguise?

It's said that the Chinese character for the word *crisis* is the combination of two other symbols—one for the word *danger* and the other for the word *opportunity*. We all know the heart-pounding emotions that can grab us when a crisis suddenly strikes our marriage: panic, meltdown, blaming, self-pity, and denial. Yet a crisis is also an opportunity for God to display His power and glory.

If we are facing a potential calamity today, we need to call out to God in prayer, asking Him to keep our focus as a couple on the truly important (God and each other) rather than the truly urgent (the crisis at hand). Someday, looking back on the crisis, we may discover that God's true agenda in that difficult hour was to bring a new maturity in our walk of faith And we can thank God for the lessons learned.

*Lord Jesus, while no crisis seems pleasant at the moment, we do believe that in difficult moments we have an opportunity to grow closer to You. Let us seize that opportunity. Amen.*

*"Sin is crouching at your door; it desires to
have you, but you must rule over it."*

GENESIS 4:7

Who triggers anger in us?

Do we recognize this scenario? The wrong word or inflection in someone's voice or a simple mistake causes someone we know to go over the top in anger. When the heat finally subsides, everyone is left wondering, *Why did that happen again?*

One pastor traces inappropriate anger in Scripture back to unresolved bitterness, moral impurity, unrealistic expectations, an idol of materialism, and self-focus. What all these causes have in common is one word: *sin.* Hurtful anger is our sinful human nature expressing itself in a way injurious to others and offensive to God.

In Genesis, God warned Cain that ungodly anger was crouching at the door of his life and desired complete control. Cain ignored the warning and eventually murdered his brother Abel. Regardless of the trigger that sets off anger, the true cause is sin that resides within our hearts. Only the presence of Christ living within us can remove such rage before it ruins our life.

*Dear Jesus, keep us in right relationship with
You so that unrighteous anger will never gain
a foothold in our life. Amen.*

*Above all, love each other deeply, because*
*love covers over a multitude of sins.*

1 PETER 4:8

What locks a human heart from giving or receiving love?

God gave us all a capacity to give and receive love. However, when our hearts are damaged, they will lock up. Author John Regier believes there are several causes of a locked heart, and most of these occur in childhood: perfectionism, impossible demands imposed on us, lack of love and attention, rejection, abandonment, and abuse. The result is a block in the ability to give and receive love.

Such heart damage is often well-disguised and may go unnoticed until marriage. Marriage requires emotional, spiritual, and physical intimacy to succeed, so a damaged heart that cannot give or receive love cannot offer intimacy either.

But there is good news. Whenever we choose to genuinely care about the heart damage in our spouse's life, and reach out in love rather than judgment, it can begin to unlock their heart. As the Scripture promises, when we love a person deeply from the heart, it covers over a multitude of sins, including the pain of the past.

*Dear Jesus, thank You that You can take*
*a heart of stone and create a heart of flesh.*
*Amen.*

*"For I hate divorce!" says the LORD, the God of
Israel. "To divorce your wife is to overwhelm her
with cruelty," says the LORD of Heaven's Armies. "So
guard your heart; do not be unfaithful to your wife."*

MALACHI 2:16 NLT

Why isn't divorce the best option to solve our problems?

Imagine that you had severe arthritis in your ankle. The pain is so intense you can't sleep. Now imagine a doctor who examines the problem and announces, "I can take that pain away forever."

"Really," you say. "Then please, by all means do it."

"Fine," the doctor says. "Let's set a date to amputate your leg."

Using divorce to solve the pain in our marriage can be much like using amputation to heal the hurt in our ankle—it creates more problems than it solves. That's why God says, "I hate divorce!" He hates the hurt and damage divorce does to us. God offers us a better alternative: learning to love one another again and discovering the higher and hidden reasons He brought us together—a far better alternative than severing the marriage for all time.

*Lord Jesus, guard us in our spirit so that we do
not break faith with one another. Amen.*

*Let love and faithfulness never leave you...*
*Then you will win favor and a good name*
*in the sight of God and man.*

PROVERBS 3:3-4

How can we regain someone's trust?

As someone once observed, it takes a lifetime to gain trust but only a moment to lose it. Perhaps we have done or said something that caused someone to lose trust in us. Is there a way back?

Thankfully, the Scriptures tell us there is. It won't be easy, but if we are willing to take the following steps, trust can be regained. First, we must genuinely repent of what we did and resolve to never do it again. Next, we make a full confession to the offended person or parties. We offer no excuses for our behavior; rather take full responsibility for it. Recognize the need to restore what we have damaged and take steps of restitution wherever possible. Finally, determine to live a life going forward based on a giving attitude rather than a taking one. It helps to have an accountability partner who walks with us through this process of regaining lost trust.

*Heavenly Father, let love and faithfulness*
*never leave us that we might gain favor from*
*You and from others. Amen.*

*Accept one another, then, just as Christ accepted*
*you, in order to bring praise to God.*

Romans 15:7

Are we stepping on each other's pain?

Why is it that we can have the same argument over and over with our spouse or relative or another person? One author believes it's because we accidentally (or perhaps deliberately) step on each other's emotional pain. By that we mean putting pressure on another person's heart where there is preexisting damage or hurt. This prior pain occurred when someone in our past forced us to meet their unrealistic expectations, controlled or dominated us, or left us feeling neglected or abandoned. Now, as adults, when someone does something similar to the hurts we experienced in our past, they are stepping on our pain.

The opposite of stepping on pain is accepting one another—just as Christ has accepted us. That means putting away our attitudes and words that may pressure another person and replacing them with words of affirmation, value, and love.

*Lord Jesus, Your kind and unconditional*
*acceptance of us has been a life-changing*
*experience. Help us to accept one another in*
*exactly the same way. Amen.*

*Love never fails.*

1 Corinthians 13:8

Are we willing to show amazing grace to our spouse? We're all likely familiar with the hymn "Amazing Grace," written by John Newton. Newton was a former slavetrader who experienced the profound and life-changing mercy of Jesus Christ. This onetime reprobate was so transformed by God's amazing grace that eventually he became a chaplain to the queen of England.

Are we willing to show this same amazing undeserved favor to those closest to us? Grace cannot be earned or merited or it is no longer grace. Grace is offering those who offend us the gift of forgiveness and love. Grace is lived out in our everyday lives when we return patience and kindness for irritation and rudeness. Grace happens when we offer compliments and affirmation in the face of unkind remarks and rejection. Grace comes alive when we show courtesy and respect in return for discourtesy and insult.

Grace is rooted in God's unending love, and His love never fails.

*Dear Jesus, amazing grace, how sweet the sound, that saved wretches like us. We once were lost, but now we're found, were blind but now we see. Let us extend that same grace to those who need it today. Amen.*

*When I was a child, I talked like a child, I thought
like a child, I reasoned like a child. When I became
a man, I put the ways of childhood behind me.*

1 Corinthians 13:11

Is it possible for us to quit fighting?

It's true. We can reach a place in our marriage where
most painful arguments end and ongoing peace prevails.
This can be true in our other close relationships as well.
How do we put an end to fighting?

Begin by agreeing that bickering, quarreling, and
name-calling are unworthy behaviors. Then ask the
other person's forgiveness for past fighting. Concur that
loving each other is far more important than winning a
fight. Agree that when a disagreement arises, we will listen and seek to understand our spouse's perspective and
then search for areas of mutual agreement. If we feel anger
growing too strong we agree to revisit the issue at hand
later.

Scripture reminds us, "When I became a man, I put
the ways of childhood behind me." Paul explains that
Christlike love is patient, kind, and does not demand its
own way. To act otherwise is childish.

*Heavenly Father, may continually showing
Christ-like love to one another be more
important to us than having our way. Amen.*

*"Moses permitted you to divorce your wives
because your hearts were hard. But it was
not this way from the beginning."*

MATTHEW 19:8

What does it mean to have a softened heart?
Jesus tells us why marriages dissolve. It is not our
lack of communication, or problems with our finances,
or even differing values. These are merely the fruit of the
problem, not the root of the problem. He says *a hardened
heart* causes divorce.

There is good news in that statement. If a hardened
heart causes us to divorce one another, then a softened
heart will open the way to our reconciliation. What is a
softened heart? It's a heart released from sin and healed by
love. If two people turn to Jesus and ask Him to forgive
the sin and heal the pain in their hearts, He will answer.

Two softened hearts can resolve any problem. It is only
a matter of when, not if, they will reconcile. Are we ready
for such a wonderful heart transplant?

*Dear Jesus, thank You for telling us the cause
and cure of our marriage problems. Soften our
hearts toward each other and keep them that
way. Amen.*

*"I will give you a new heart and put a new
spirit in you; I will remove from you your
heart of stone and give you a heart of flesh."*

EZEKIEL 36:26

Would we like a soft heart?

The world was stunned when the first heart transplant took place in the late 1960s. How could the heart of one human being be placed in another? Yet a far greater miracle occurs whenever a spiritual heart that has been hardened by sin and resentment is replaced by one filled with love and forgiveness.

According to Scripture, God is in the business of performing such heart transplants. Ezekiel says God will remove our heart of stone and replace it with a heart of flesh. How can God perform this miracle? First, we must ask Him to do a thorough inner heart exam. We must confess every area of sin He exposes in our heart. Then we must invite His Holy Spirit to fill our heart with the love of Jesus. The result will be a new heart with all the vital signs of a disciple of Jesus Christ.

*Lord Jesus, replace our stony and unloving
heart with a soft and caring heart—a heart
like Yours. Amen.*

*On the third day a wedding took
place at Cana in Galilee…
What Jesus did here [changing water into wine] was
the first of the signs through which he revealed his glory.*

JOHN 2:1,11

Can a loving marriage win people to Christ?

Jesus chose to first reveal He was the Son of God at a wedding, of all places. While He could have performed His first miracle in a crowded marketplace or before religious leaders in the inner courts of the Temple, He chose instead to use a small wedding in an obscure village in Galilee. Why such an unlikely choice? Jesus wanted to make a statement that marriage symbolizes God's desired relationship with us—the relationship that Jesus came to establish by His death and resurrection.

We seldom appreciate the impact a loving marriage can have on others around us—particularly those who don't know Jesus as their Savior. Yet, a loving marriage ultimately points to the love relationship between Christ and His Church. Loving marriages become an evangelistic tool to preach the Good News of Jesus Christ and to reveal His glory.

*Dear Lord, please make our marriage a living
witness of Your love for Your church and the
honor Your church has for you. Amen.*

*It is God's will that...each of you should learn to
control your own body in a way that is holy and
honorable, not in passionate lust like the pagans, who
do not know God; and that in this matter no one
should wrong or take advantage of a brother or sister.*

1 Thessalonians 4:3-6

What does it mean to take advantage of a person of
the opposite sex?

One author has described how men and women
can take advantage of each other. Men take advantage
of women by touching, caressing, and suggestive talk.
Women take advantage of men by eye language, suggestive manner of dress, and flirting. Eventually such behavior can lead to sexual sin, a lack of genuine love, and even
hatred for the other person. If we are a believer, acting in
this way ultimately destroys God's reputation.

Through the power of the indwelling Holy Spirit, we
can learn to control our own bodies and view others as
individuals of great value in the eyes of God. We can relate
to them with holiness and honor. We are to live in the
truth and never wrong or take advantage of another.

*Dear Jesus, make us aware of our responsibility
toward each other and keep us from willful sin.
May we guard Your holy reputation and name.
Amen.*

*Praise be to the God and Father of our Lord Jesus
Christ…For he chose us in him before the creation
of the world to be holy and blameless in his sight. In
love he predestined us for adoption to sonship through
Jesus Christ, in accordance with his pleasure and will.*

EPHESIANS 1:3-5

Do we suffer from low self-esteem?

In their insightful book *Building Your Mate's Self-Esteem*, Dennis and Barbara Rainey list several clues for spotting our low self-esteem. Perhaps our childhood was marked by parental abuse, neglect, ignorance, or overbearing authority. Or we now fear opening up, being real and vulnerable. Or perhaps we get discouraged easily or have difficulty admitting wrong or always need to be right. And finally, we may find it difficult to forgive.

All these characteristics point to a person who wasn't raised to understand their eternal value and significance to God. Our Father God chose us in Christ before the creation of the world to be adopted as His children. To know that God has wanted us before time began is the ultimate source of self-esteem.

*Heavenly Father, praise be to Your name now
and forever for choosing us to be welcomed
into Your forever family. Amen.*

*For the wages of sin is death, but the gift of
God is eternal life in Christ Jesus our Lord.*

Romans 6:23

What are some widely held lies about sexual sin?

Erwin Lutzer, pastor of Moody Memorial Church in Chicago, lists five lies we tell ourselves about sexual sin: (1) If it's beautiful it must be right; (2) I'm entitled to whatever makes me happy; (3) Because God understands how I'm made, He overlooks my sin; (4) I can manage the consequences of my sin; and (5) I am locked into my lifestyle and there is no way out.

The only way to defeat any lie is with the truth. That liberating truth is found in God's Word. The Bible teaches that all sin, even when it appears to be beautiful, still leads to death. Scripture tells us we are not entitled to happiness, only to a life of obedience. It warns that God cannot overlook sin, but must judge it. Finally, it advises that the consequences of sin will control us, not the other way around.

Refuse to believe the lies, no matter how widely held.

*Heavenly Father, keep us from deceptions
that would ruin our life, and let the full and
bright light of Your truth shine daily upon our
lives. Amen.*

*May I never boast except in the cross of our
Lord Jesus Christ, through which the world
has been crucified to me, and I to the world.*

GALATIANS 6:14

What can the cross of Christ teach us about marriage?
The most well-known symbol of Christianity is
the cross, and it contains valuable lessons for our married
lives. The cross teaches us we are all sinful human beings
and that we can treat each other very badly. The cross
teaches that forgiveness is costly and required the sacrifice of God's one and only Son. Applied to marriage that
means forgiving our spouse can be difficult, requiring we
die to self in order to extend pardon. The cross teaches that
mercy has the final word, which means as justified as we
may be in our anger, mercy must triumph over judgment
for our relationship to flourish.

Finally, the cross teaches that we can start all over
again, meaning a fresh start may be needed. Thankfully
the power of Christ's forgiveness will always be available
for us to do just that.

*Lord Jesus, if things become difficult between
us, may Your cross be our example and
motivation to forgive each other as we have
been forgiven. Amen.*

*Do not be yoked together with unbelievers…*
*What does a believer have in common*
*with an unbeliever?*

2 Corinthians 6:14-15

L ooking for some good advice for our children?
     All of us want our children to grow up and marry
well. Part of our responsibility as parents is to warn them in
advance of danger signs in a potential mate. These bright
yellow caution lights include: (1) someone currently struggling with an addiction of any kind, (2) someone who
leaves behind them a litter of broken relationships, (3)
someone who asks you to sleep with them before you are
married, (4) someone who plans their day only to please
themselves, and (5) someone who doesn't share your faith
in Jesus Christ.

     The time to teach these principles is while our children
are still growing up, but even as adults we still owe our
children the truth. Don't be afraid to speak God's warning into our children's lives regardless of their age. While
they may not receive it right now, someday they will thank
us for it.

*Dear Jesus, thank You that God's Word*
*gives us clear and practical advice regarding*
*relationships. May we share that wisdom with*
*our children in a spirit of love and*
*humility. Amen.*

*And that is what some of you were. But you were washed, you were sanctified, you were justified in the name of the Lord Jesus Christ and by the Spirit of our God.*

1 Corinthians 6:11

What hope is there for breaking addictions?

One of the most devastating heartbreaks in marriage is dealing with an addition, whether our own or our spouse's. Christ can offer the addict a radical change of identity, a radical inner transformation of beliefs, and a radical power surge of freedom. Once a person realizes their true identity is in Christ, not the particular addiction they struggle with, they can receive fresh hope. Once they comprehend the lies that they believed about themselves and God, the power of deception can be broken. Once they experience the presence of the Holy Spirit, they can experience power to walk free again.

The Scriptures testify to the reality of transformation, "And that is what some of you were. But you were washed..." Are we ready to move from what we were to what we could be in Jesus?

*Lord Jesus, thank You that You offer freedom from whatever habit has taken us captive. Wash, sanctify, and justify us in Your Name. Amen.*

*Now when Jesus saw the crowds, he went up
on a mountainside and sat down. His disciples
came to him, and he began to teach them.*

Matthew 5:1-2

Can the Sermon on the Mount help our marriage?

If we were to approach Jesus for help with our marriage, what portions of Scripture might He point us to? One likely place is His Sermon on the Mount. It offers timely and practical counsel easily applied to marriage.

For example, we should not kill our love with anger or call each other names we'll later regret. Don't go to worship until we've apologized and attempted reconciliation. Don't give other women (or men) a second look or use divorce to settle our problems. Don't return evil for evil or treat our spouse like an enemy.

Why don't we begin working through this wonderful sermon together and applying the principles Jesus teaches to our marriage issues? As He says at the conclusion of His sermon, "Everyone who hears these words of mine and puts them into practice is like a wise man who built his house on the rock."

*Master and Lord, build our house on the
solid rock of Your wisdom and counsel so that
regardless of the great storms of life, our house
will stand strong. Amen.*

*"In your anger do not sin."*
EPHESIANS 4:26

How is it possible to be angry yet not sin?

We have all experienced a thoughtless word carelessly spoken, a foolish choice impulsively made, or an insensitive attitude casually displayed toward us. All these things can provoke anger within us. When that happens, we have the choice to utilize the anger that leads to sin or to use the anger that does not lead to sin. Sinful anger brims with thoughts of retaliation, punishment, and even hate. Healthy anger, as Gary Chapman points out, motivates us to take constructive action to resolve the offense in a godly way.

How then can we be angry yet not sin? We should use our distress to turn our attention toward addressing the problem before us. While we confront the offense head-on, we do so in a spirit of love, self-control, and truthfulness. If we are successful in resolving the issue, the relationship can return to normal. If we are not able to come to agreement, we then surrender it to God and patiently wait for reconciliation to occur while maintaining a spirit of love and forbearance.

*Lord Jesus, let our anger always be under the*
*control of the Holy Spirit that it may resolve*
*our relationships rather than destroy them.*
*Amen.*

*Therefore each of you must put off falsehood*
*and speak truthfully to your neighbor, for*
*we are all members of one body.*

EPHESIANS 4:25

Is telling the truth good or bad for a marriage?

We've heard the old adage, "The truth hurts." That's why many couples avoid sharing what's actually going on inside their hearts and minds. They reason it's better to keep such painful thoughts to themselves rather than risk a confrontation.

While not every upsetting notion needs to be spoken and not every troubling emotion requires expression (maturity demands just the opposite), consistently hiding our true feelings and thoughts from one another exacts a high price. Our spouse can assume the marriage is doing just fine while we are inwardly languishing. Worse yet, absent the truth we may never come to know true intimacy or resolve real hurts.

While the truth can hurt, it can also heal—when spoken in love. That's why the Bible encourages each of us to "put off falsehood and speak truthfully to [our] neighbor." That's particularly important when that neighbor is our spouse.

*Heavenly Father, help us to walk daily in Your*
*truth, that we might know true fellowship*
*and love for one another. Amen.*

*Do not let the sun go down while you are still angry.*

Ephesians 4:26

How long should we let an argument go on? Have we ever gone to sleep still upset with each other? The Bible says that's not a good idea. We'll wake up knowing that things are not right—and that's a truly horrible way to start the day. The longer we put off resolving the disagreement, the more intense our emotions will grow, which makes resolving the problem even more difficult.

How can we put away our anger before sundown? We should take the initiative in approaching the other person to discuss what is disturbing us. We can use "I" statements such as, "I felt humiliated when you made fun of what I was wearing in front of your family." We must allow the other person an opportunity to apologize or clarify what they meant, or both. Even if they do not ask for it, we should choose to offer words of forgiveness.

If further reconciliation is necessary, pursue it by agreeing to continue the discussion the next day. But by all means leave your anger behind with the setting sun.

*Lord Jesus, motivate us to resolve our issues*
*before we go to sleep so that today's anger will*
*not consume tomorrow's joy. Amen.*

*And do not give the devil a foothold.*
EPHESIANS 4:27

If you give the devil an inch, will he take a mile?

Bob grew up with a Labrador German shepherd dog that slept on his bed. At first the family pet occupied just a little space on the mattress. But over time, he grew larger and larger until he took over most of Bob's twin bed. Many nights Bob ended up sleeping on about an eight-inch-wide portion of the mattress.

Unhealthy anger operates like that greedy dog. It starts out taking up only small portions of our heart—but over time it demands more and more of our territory. Finally, the day arrives when it owns us outright.

Can we think back on issues that were once relatively small and insignificant, but over time grew in intensity and scope? What may have started out as a toehold eventually became a foothold, then an arm hold, and finally a stranglehold on our hearts.

It may be time to ask God to free us from anger's terrible grip.

*Heavenly Father, forgive us for nursing small*
*resentments and giving the devil a foothold.*
*We cancel the ground we gave to him and*
*return it to the rightful lordship of Jesus Christ.*
*Amen.*

*Do not let any unwholesome talk
come out of your mouths.*

EPHESIANS 4:29

Are certain words off limits in a marriage?
"I hate you." "I've never loved you." "I wish you were dead." "I want a divorce." These soul-searing words should never leave our mouths. While a marriage can recover from such devastating statements, the scars sometimes remain for months or even years.

That's why we should make a solemn promise to each other—on a day when things are calm and the relationship is going well—that we will never utter certain phrases and words no matter how upset, disappointed, or brokenhearted we may be at the moment. Such toxic and devastating utterances are out-of-bounds for the rest of our lives.

If we have spoken such words in the past, today is the day to ask forgiveness and to commit to never speaking them again. When the Bible says don't let any unwholesome talk come out of our mouths, it means just that.

*Heavenly Father, place our tongues and the
words they speak under the daily control and
direction of the Author of the words of life—
our Lord Jesus. Amen.*

*[Say] only what is helpful for building
others up according to their needs, that
it may benefit those who listen.*

EPHESIANS 4:29

Are our words a construction or demolition crew?
When it comes to buildings, there are basically two
types of workers—those who build them and those who
tear them down. The same is true of the words we use
in marriage. Either our words build up the self-esteem,
value, and dignity of our spouse, or they tear the person
down. A loving marriage is carefully constructed each day
by choosing thoughtfully what we say, infusing our words
with kindness, sensitivity, and wisdom.

We have tried to follow this helpful rule: anything that
needs to be said should be said with kindness. There is
no difficult topic or incident that cannot be discussed in
a spirit of gentleness and kindness. Scripture commands
us to say only what is helpful and beneficial to others,
including our spouse. Everything that does not build up
becomes a wrecking ball that tears down our relationships.

*Lord Jesus, let the words of our mouth and the
meditations of our heart be pleasing in Your
sight, O Lord our Rock and Redeemer. Amen.*

*God sets the lonely in families…*
*but the rebellious live in a sun-scorched land.*

PSALM 68:6

Is our heart in rebellion?

Rebellion occurs whenever we react against the legitimate authorities God places in our lives. If we rebel against our parents, God, and others, we will eventually carry that same attitude into our marriage. Symptoms of rebellion include constant arguing, prevailing tension, and a lack of desire for intimacy.

One author believes that walking the road of rebellion follows a predictable pattern. First, the rebellious person sets up their own system of morality. They themselves decide, not God's Word, what is right and wrong. Then calamity strikes their lives. God puts pressure on their lives to break their rebellion. Finally, the rebellious come to a place of despair. They realize that by sowing rebellion, they are reaping only negative consequences.

If our heart is in rebellion, we need to confess that as sin and seek God's forgiveness. We may also need to apologize to our spouse and children. Rebellion breeds loneliness while submission to God builds loving relationships.

*Lord Jesus, forgive us for the hidden rebellion*
*in our heart. We fully submit to Your lordship*
*in our lives. Amen.*

*Don't you know that when you offer yourselves to
someone as obedient slaves, you are slaves of the one
you obey—whether you are slaves to sin, which leads
to death, or to obedience, which leads to righteousness?*

ROMANS 6:16

What's wrong with pornography?

Some argue that pornography is relatively harmless. Others claim it can actually be good for a marriage. The truth is quite the opposite. Study after study has demonstrated that pornography lowers our commitment to our marriage. It diminishes our interest in our wife. It is a progressive addiction leading to more and more sordid images. It directs our powerful emotions and thoughts to someone we are not married to.

That's why the Bible says that to look on a woman with lust in our hearts is the same as committing adultery. Clearly, adultery is destructive to our soul and spirit. How do we find freedom from visual adultery? The Scriptures tell us we are to offer ourselves as slaves to obedience to God. That requires daily a complete surrender of our will to the will of Jesus Christ.

*Lord Jesus, make us pure in heart that we
might desire to see God rather than sinful
images. Amen.*

*"The bride belongs to the bridegroom. The friend who attends the bridegroom waits and listens for him, and is full of joy when he hears the bridegroom's voice."*

JOHN 3:29

Are there positive ways to get your husband to talk?

It's a common complaint among wives—"My husband just won't talk to me." Let us suggest some strategies that will get him talking, and some that won't. Here are some strategies that are doomed to failure: Nagging him. Following him around the house repeating issues. Setting up "summit meetings."

But doing an activity together for thirty minutes each day will work. Listening to his thoughts without criticizing him will work. Asking him caring questions and patiently waiting for him to answer, regardless of how much silence may intervene, will work.

In ancient Israel the friend of the bridegroom eagerly awaited his arrival, filled with joy when at last he heard the bridegroom's voice. That's a good idea for brides to practice as well—waiting patiently to hear his voice and rejoicing when you do.

*Lord Jesus, teach us to ask sincere and loving questions, and then show the respect and courtesy to await the answer with patience and love. Amen.*

*Fools mock at making amends for sin,
but goodwill is found among the upright.*

PROVERBS 14:9

Who should be the first to apologize?

In his insightful book *Love and Respect,* Emerson Eggerichs explains that many arguments between spouses are the result of confused messages. The wife feels she was treated with a lack of love. The husband feels he was treated with a lack of respect. Both feel the other should apologize first. When asked who he believes should take the initiative in making an apology, Dr. Eggerichs replies (with no doubt a wry smile), "The one who is the more mature."

In a healthy marriage, each spouse should take the initiative to admit they may have misread their spouse's motives. The Bible teaches that only fools mock at the idea of making amends for sin, but goodwill is found among the upright. When our marriage relationship is disrupted by acrimony and argument, so is our relationship with Christ. To resolve the first problem in love and humility is to restore the second in righteousness and obedience.

*Precious Savior, create in our hearts not only
willingness but an eagerness to restore the
harmony to our marriage relationship
when it is lost. Amen.*

*"Blessed are the meek,
for they will inherit the earth."*

Matthew 5:5

Is meekness an invitation to be walked on?

Many people misunderstand the nature of meekness. They believe it is weakness and abdication, requiring them to lose every argument or to give up every personal conviction to please others. Nothing could be further from the truth. Meekness is far from pathetic weakness or cowering subservience. It is renouncing our prideful self-focus and keeping our strength under God's control.

Jesus exemplified meekness when He was willing to suffer death upon the cross. He compromised nothing of His character or personhood or commitment to the truth, only the temptation to use His divine strength to control others. The result was that God exalted Jesus to a place that is above every other name.

When we make the decision to abandon our self-will and put our strength under God's control, the life-giving blessings of heaven will begin to flow into our lives. Meekness transforms our marriage into a porch light for blessing, not a doormat for exploitation.

*Lord Jesus, may we be willing to walk the
same road of meekness You walked, that God's
will be done in our lives as it is in heaven.
Amen.*

*"Blessed are those who mourn,*
*for they will be comforted."*

Matthew 5:4

Is there such a thing as good grief?

Grief is an emotion most of us would rather avoid. It is most often associated with the death of a loved one or a searing personal loss. Yet not all grief in Scripture is associated with death and deprivation. In the Sermon on the Mount, Jesus says those who mourn are actually blessed.

He's referring to the deep sorrow and regret we need to feel over our sinful condition. We should recognize the heartbreaking impact our disobedience has on God, others, and our own life. Once we see the awfulness of our sin and its deep offensiveness to God, the door swings open to receiving God's redeeming comfort. We see with new clarity the grace of the Lord Jesus Christ and His offer of full forgiveness. Mourning over sin becomes the road to rejoicing over pardon. We should pity those who never mourn for their sins, for they have missed the blessing of good grief.

*Lord Jesus, thank You for the convicting power*
*of the Holy Spirit. Only when we understand*
*how bad the bad news really is of our sinfulness*
*can we see how good the Good News truly is*
*of your salvation. Amen.*

*"Blessed are those who hunger and
thirst for righteousness,
for they will be filled."*

MATTHEW 5:6

Is it a blessing to go hungry and thirsty?

Have we ever been famished, opened our refrigerator, and found it empty? Or come in on a hot day dreaming about a bottle of ice cold water only to find someone drank the last one? Then we know firsthand that hunger and thirst are not much fun.

Yet, the right kind of famishment and thirstiness can become among the most satisfying experiences in life. Jesus said, "Blessed are those who hunger and thirst…for righteousness." While the word *righteousness* can carry a variety of meanings, at its core it is simply being right with God and each other in our conduct, character, and concerns.

Jesus calls us to an intense inner desire to be done with sin and filled with what is right. When God encounters such a noble desire in our hearts, He responds by freely sharing His Spirit with us. He meets the deepest longings of our hearts for holiness and satisfies our hunger and thirst for righteousness as nothing else can—that's real blessing.

*Dear Jesus, create in us holy famishment and
thirst for right living and relationships. Amen.*

*"Blessed are the merciful,*
*for they will be shown mercy."*

MATTHEW 5:7

Should we give others what they deserve or what they need?

It's hard to be gracious when we feel like returning "an eye for an eye and a tooth for a tooth." However, Jesus calls us to a higher standard, urging us to show mercy instead of doling out judgment. His reasoning is simple: if we show mercy to others, then we will be shown mercy ourselves.

The longer we live the more we should become aware of our inherent frailties, weaknesses, and sinfulness. When a woman was about to be stoned to death for her act of adultery, Jesus invited the ones without sin to cast the first stone. Ironically, the oldest members of the group put down their rocks first. In the moral and spiritual universe that God has created, those who demonstrate mercy are the ones who can expect to receive it. He promises it so.

Shakespeare was right when he wrote, "The quality of mercy is never strained."

*Heavenly Father, remind us that we are the*
*recipients of Your great mercy demonstrated in*
*the cross of Jesus Christ. May we in turn share*
*that same mercy with others. Amen.*

*"Blessed are the pure in heart,
for they will see God."*
Matthew 5:8

Have we caught a glimpse of God's face lately?

The Bible tells us that no one can see the face of God and live. Even the great spiritual figures of the Old Testament trembled at the idea of seeing Almighty God face-to-face. His intense holiness and purity is too much for sinful mortal man to behold and still live.

However, in the New Testament, God walked among us in Jesus Christ. He taught His disciples they could see God if their hearts were pure. Holiness of heart opens the door to a close and personal glimpse of God's character. His pure heart connects with our pure heart as we see Him at work in our lives.

For some husbands that may mean erasing the pornography on a computer and trashing explicit DVDs. For wives it may mean curbing the tongue and refusing to use cell phones or e-mail as gossip machines. Purity in heart allows God's face to shine in all its brilliance in your home, relationships, and marriage.

*Dear Jesus, remove everything from our lives
that would hide Your glorious face. Amen.*

*"Blessed are the peacemakers,*
*for they will be called children of God."*

MATTHEW 5:9

What's wrong with being a peacekeeper?

Are we the one in a relationship always to smooth things over? Do we quickly take the blame if someone is angry—even if we're not to blame? Is our unstated goal in life peace at any price? If so, that's called peacekeeping. Though on the surface it appears noble and sacrificial, in the end it will wear us out and damage our relationships. Worse yet, we may one day flip and become an aggressive, domineering, and angry person—now a peace-breaker.

The Bible calls us not to be peacekeepers but peacemakers. What's the difference? Peacemaking is taking on the task of confronting tough issues, speaking the whole truth in love, and tenaciously working together to find a solution. It is, as one author put it, "risking chaos to achieve community."

Jesus promises a special reward for peacemakers— they will be called "children of God." Why? Our heavenly Father is the ultimate Peacemaker.

*Dear Jesus, thank You for making peace*
*between God and man on the cross. We desire*
*to share that peace with others and be called*
*Your sons and daughters. Amen.*

*"Blessed are those who are persecuted*
*because of righteousness,*
*for theirs is the kingdom of heaven."*

MATTHEW 5:10

Are we treated wrong because we try to live right?

It can be discouraging to be in a relationship where those close to us don't share our spiritual values. They may ridicule or subtly punish us for our faith. They may be constantly looking for inconsistencies in our words or behavior. It would be easy to just give up trying to live out our faith before them.

God has a much better alternative than abdication—it's patient endurance. Patience is gained by asking the Holy Spirit to manifest His fruit in our lives, while endurance is won by keeping our eyes on Jesus, the Author and Finisher of our faith. Together they produce a precious character trait that Jesus has promised to reward. Whatever He might have in mind for the persecutor, He is preparing us for our eternal residence in the kingdom of God. That kingdom is both present right now and is coming in the future.

Don't give up. There is a blessing coming our way.

*Lord Jesus, may we remember we are blessed*
*when we are in trouble because of our*
*faithfulness to You. Amen.*

*"Blessed are you when people insult you,
persecute you and falsely say all kinds
of evil against you because of me."*

MATTHEW 5:11

Is living for God becoming too costly?

Believers who come from non-Christian backgrounds can find themselves at odds with their closest relatives. Parents can put pressure on us to stay away from church or tone down our witness. Siblings can laugh at the way we're raising our kids or educating them. That can leave wounds, discouragement, and frustration.

Yet the Bible says we are not to despair when we are insulted or persecuted. We need to realize that Jesus endured the same difficulties we do. At one point even His relatives thought He had lost His mind and tried to take Him home. He did not allow personal attacks to turn Him back.

God has promised to bless us if we courageously continue to follow Christ in spite of the slights or insults we endure. Jesus has counted us worthy to share in His sufferings. It's a sign we are living as we should and that our testimony is real.

*Dear Jesus, help us to remember that if we
share in Your sufferings, one day we shall also
share in Your glory. Amen.*

*"Let your light shine before others, that they may see
your good deeds and glorify your Father in heaven."*

MATTHEW 5:16

Are we leaving the light on at home?

We all look for ways to save energy and cut our utility bills. Turning off the lights when we leave the room or dialing down the thermostat when we're away just make sense. And yet, we should allow some lights in our lives to burn both day and night. These are the lights of good deeds motivated by our love for God. These loving acts can be as simple as holding the door open for an elderly couple or as dramatic as offering to donate a kidney for a friend who will die without a match.

Our world is filled with the darkness of selfishness, greed, and apathy. That's why the believer who performs good deeds shines with a loving radiance that others notice. Even the cynical and doubting among us have to acknowledge our Father in heaven. Keeping the light on in our lives will bring glory to God.

*Dear Jesus, give us opportunity this day to
bring light to some person's darkness. Shine
through us in simple acts of kindness and love.
Amen.*

*"You are the salt of the earth. But if the salt loses
its saltiness, how can it be made salty again?"*

MATTHEW 5:13

Does our marriage need a dash of salt?

Salt is the one spice that's on almost everyone's table. It brings out hidden flavor, preserves food from spoiling, and creates in us a healthy thirst. Jesus says the quality of our hearts is like salt—it improves the flavor of our relationship, preserves our love from spoiling, and creates a healthy thirst for more of God. Yet, Jesus warns that our salt can lose its saltiness. How can that happen?

When we grow tired and apathetic and quit pursuing our relationship with Christ, our saltiness begins to diminish. When we let unforgiveness and bitterness take over our hearts, we start to lose saltiness. When we wander into known and willful sin, our saltiness begins to disappear.

To maintain saltiness we must walk daily close to God in loving trust and obedience. The result is our faith is spiced with vitality, our hearts are free of resentment, and our daily lives are marked by purity and holiness.

*Lord Jesus, make and keep us the salt of the
earth for as long as both shall live. Amen.*

*Many [spouses] claim to have unfailing love,*
*but a faithful [spouse] who can find?*

PROVERBS 20:6

Is our marriage really our top priority?

When couples complain, "Our marriage is unsatisfying," they often don't realize they have starved their marriage to death with the lack of time and attention. We read once that the average married couple spends only three to five minutes a day in personal, intimate conversation. That's as much time as we sometimes spend waiting for an older computer to boot up.

If we are going to make our marriage our top priority, we should ask, "How much time am I willing to invest in my marriage today?" Whatever is at the top of our to-do list on our smartphone or computer, we should consider erasing it and writing instead, "Spend thirty minutes with my spouse." At the end of the week, we ought to do a time audit to determine if we have spent at least ten hours with our spouse in unhurried, focused, and quality time. If not, it's time to seriously rearrange our priorities.

*Lord Jesus, may we love and value our*
*relationship with You and our spouse and*
*demonstrate our commitment by the time*
*we spend together each day. Amen.*

*Why, you do not even know what will happen
tomorrow. What is your life? You are a mist that
appears for a little while and then vanishes.*

JAMES 4:14

Remember, our marriage comes with an expiration date.
Even if we are married for a lifetime, it is still "until
death do us part." Even if God should grant you fifty or
sixty or even seventy years together, those years will one
day come to an end.

The great preacher Vance Havner suggests we should
treat each day as if it were the first day of our marriage—
look forward to it. Then treat each day as if it were the best
day of our marriage—enjoy it. Finally, treat each day as if
it were the last day of our marriage—treasure it.

The Bible reminds us that we don't even know what
will happen tomorrow. But we do have today, and by
God's grace we can value our marriage for the gift it truly is.

Yes, even the best of marriages comes with an expiration date.

*Heavenly Father, may we keep the end of life
in mind that we might truly enjoy each day
for the present it is. Amen.*

*The wise woman builds her house,*
*but with her own hands the foolish one tears hers down.*

PROVERBS 14:1

If our husband shared important secrets about himself, what might they be?

Shaunti Feldhahn, in her excellent book *For Women Only: What You Need to Know About the Inner Lives of Men,* shares several things your husband wants you to understand about him. Among them are these: he would rather feel unloved than feel disrespected; he feels insecure about carrying the burden of being the provider; he enjoys romance but doubts his romantic skills; and he loves you but sometimes doesn't know how to say it.

Wives, this calls for patience and understanding on our part. Because we value love over respect, we may not see why respect is so important to him. Because he enjoys his work, we may not pick up on his fear of failing to provide. Because his romantic skills don't come easily, we need to avoid labeling it a lack of interest. Finally, just because he may not say "I love you" as often as he feels it, we should not interpret it as a lack of love.

*Gracious Lord, may we as husbands and wives*
*understand just how different we are and yet*
*how much we need the same thing—genuine*
*love. Amen.*

*Surely your goodness and love will follow me*
*all the days of my life,*
*and I will dwell in the house of the L*ORD *forever.*

PSALM 23:6

Ever wish holidays came with a survival guide?
Seasonal celebrations often add only stress and
great pressure to marriages because of forced contact with
difficult relatives, a lack of money and time, and unresolved childhood hurts. All these factors can drive our
stress levels right off the charts.

Thankfully a survival manual is found in the Twenty-
Third Psalm. There God's Word assures us we can turn to
Jesus as our Shepherd who will lead us to a place of rest,
stillness, and peace. He will lovingly direct us in the right
paths for dealing with difficult people. He will deliver us
from fear of the circumstances we are facing. He will fill
our cups to overflowing and anoint our lives with His
Spirit. And finally, we can rest in His goodness and love
that will follow all the days of our life—and that includes
the entire holiday season.

*Gentle Shepherd, make our holidays truly*
*joyous knowing that one day we shall dwell in*
*Your house forever where the celebrations will*
*never end. Amen.*

*This is a profound mystery—but I am*
*talking about Christ and the church.*

EPHESIANS 5:32

Why is marriage such a wonderful plan?

Of all the images and metaphors God could have chosen to communicate the love Christ has for the church and the honor the church has for Christ—He chose marriage. Marriage uniquely communicates the magnificent elements of God's mysterious plan to redeem the human race.

Jesus, who is pictured as the husband, lays down His very life for His bride, the church. The church as the bride responds to her husband's sacrificial giving with a spirit of honor and submission. The bride is not forced to do so, but she gladly yields in love to the overwhelming care of her husband. Together they enjoy a oneness and unity that shall exist for all eternity.

Once Jesus returns for His bride, marriage will no longer be present in heaven. It will have fulfilled its grand purpose in displaying before the universe the mystery of Christ and the church.

*Dear God, thank You that Your plan of*
*salvation is so marvelous and mysterious that*
*it will take all of eternity's day to understand*
*its depth and meaning. Amen.*

*"'Now, therefore, the sword will never depart from your house, because you despised me and took the wife of [someone else] to be your own.'"*

2 Samuel 12:10

Wh at are the insidious lies of adultery?

The tempter knows getting someone to break their sacred wedding vows is no easy task, so he uses all the weapons at his disposal to weaken defenses. He first whispers: "You deserve this because you are so special." He then offers a malevolent reassurance: "No one will ever know. This is one secret you can keep for a lifetime." He pushes further with a promise: "Don't worry, no one will get hurt nor will any permanent harm be done." His final lie: "There's no sin involved as long as you both love each other. Besides, God wants you to be happy."

The great King David learned otherwise. Though God forgave David the guilt of his sin, severe consequences were visited upon him. "The sword will never depart from your house," God said.

Sin always brings with it sad and unforeseen consequences, which is why the Lord warns us to stay way clear.

*Lord Jesus, deliver us from the voice of deception and let the Holy Spirit shout the truth in our hearts when it is needed. Amen.*

*The words of the reckless pierce like swords,*
*but the tongue of the wise brings healing.*

PROVERBS 12:18

What are some things to never do in an argument? There is much truth in the old adage, "Never say never." Yet we should never do certain things in marriage. Pastor Tommy Nelson, in his wonderful and practical *The Book of Romance*, reminds us of several "nevers" to live by in a marriage. These include: Never confront your mate publicly or in your children's presence (and never use your children in the conflict). Never win an argument through reasoning, logic, or just out-arguing the other person. Finally, never bring each other's family members into the discussion. The reason behind these "nevers" is to keep you from doing permanent damage to your marriage relationship.

The Bible reminds us that reckless or thoughtless words "pierce like swords." They can leave deep and lasting wounds in a marriage. Rather we should use our tongues to bring healing, reconciliation, and peace to our relationship.

Never forget these important principles. Never.

*Lord Jesus, set a guard over our lips and*
*a hedge around our words to prevent us*
*from saying today what we will deeply*
*regret tomorrow. Amen.*

*If we confess our sins, he is faithful and
just and will forgive us our sins and
purify us from all unrighteousness.*

1 John 1:9

Can the bondage of moral failure be broken?

What can we do if we find ourselves continually trapped in the prison of moral failure? This can include an addiction to pornography, an illicit emotional affair, or even the memory of a shameful moral failure long ago.

One pastor offers the following biblical steps to help us find freedom. First, tell God exactly how we have violated His moral values. Second, make a list of moral failures and confess each one before our heavenly Father. Third, ask God to take back the spiritual ground we gave to the enemy through our sinful actions, which give our enemy a chance to harass, accuse, and even torment us. And finally, yield that ground in our life to the lordship of Jesus Christ.

Taken together, we can break the bonds of moral failure and walk out a free person in Jesus Christ. Isn't it time to experience the sunshine of true liberty and purity in our heart?

*Lord Jesus, we thank You that for freedom You
have set us free. Amen.*

*As far as the east is from the west,*
*so far has he removed our transgressions from us.*

PSALM 103:12

How can you deal with the memory of past failures? Sometimes for years, even decades, we can continue to struggle with the burden of past immoral episodes. Though we may have asked for forgiveness a hundred times, we find no relief from the accusing voice of our past.

John Regier recommends this biblical route to putting the past in the past. After confessing our specific sins to God (which we may have done over and over), we must choose to forgive ourselves for each failure. Next, we must accept the emotional pain and consequences we have caused ourselves and others and give those consequences over to Christ to carry. Then we must yield each thought, desire, and action to Christ to experience daily moral freedom and fulfillment. Finally, we should go forward believing the promise that as far as the east is from the west, He has removed our transgressions from us.

An eternity now stands between our past guilt and our present freedom.

*Lord Jesus, may we never call anyone*
*unclean—including ourselves—that You*
*have declared clean. Amen.*

*Brothers and sisters, if someone is caught in a sin, you
who live by the Spirit should restore that person gently.
But watch yourselves, or you also may be tempted.*

GALATIANS 6:1

Are we ready to help someone break a sinful habit?
The Christian life was never intended to be lived in
isolation. We were made for community and relationships.
To enable a person to break free from sinful habits or self-
destructive behaviors may require someone to love them
and hold them responsible for their actions.

One term used in Scripture for the Holy Spirit is
"Counselor," literally "one who comes alongside." For the
Holy Spirit to set free a person who is caught in an addiction, someone else may need to come alongside. Are we
willing to be the kind of person that someone who is
caught in a sin can trust with their deepest secrets? The
kind of person who will pray and encourage them and
who will not abandon them should they temporarily
stumble?

If so, God can use us to turn a sinner from the error
of their ways and to cover over a multitude of sins. Are we
ready to be such a counselor?

*Dear Jesus, thank You that You are the
Wonderful Counselor, the Mighty God, the
Everlasting Father, and the Prince of Peace.
Amen.*

*A lying tongue hates those it hurts,*
*and a flattering mouth works ruin.*

PROVERBS 26:28

What kind of tongue do we have?

The *Life Application Study Bible* warns us that the tongue is a powerful weapon used for good or evil. It lists various types of tongues and challenges us to consider which one we have.

Consider the *controlled* tongue—do we think before we speak and know when to remain quiet? In some situations the wisest thing to do is to say nothing. The controlled tongue understands the virtues of well-chosen silence. The *caring* tongue allows us to speak the truth and encourage our spouse. Such a person uses words to affirm and build up another individual. The *conniving* tongue is bent on gossip, slander, and twisting the truth. Words are used to cause harm, shame, and embarrassment to others. Finally, the *careless* tongue can lie, curse, and use quick-tempered words.

The Bible says the tongue has the power of life and death. For which purpose will we use our tongue today?

*Our heavenly Father, it is not right that*
*with the same tongue we should bless and we*
*should curse. Bring our words under the*
*control and direction of the Holy Spirit. Amen.*

*"First take the plank out of your own
eye, and then you will see clearly to remove
the speck from your [spouse's] eye."*

MATTHEW 7:5

What if a spouse just doesn't care anymore?

In struggling marriages, one person is usually trying harder than the other to reconcile. Gary Chapman, marriage and family-life author and speaker, has solid advice for spouses whose partner seems to have detached from the marriage. First, resist the temptation to judge the other person. Look for the real issues in their life, such as low self-esteem, past wounds, and unmet needs. Finding the reasons why the person shuts down and withdraws is critical. Offer them support and praise in the areas where they perform well. No one is a complete failure, and finding places to affirm can draw out the best in them. Ask them each month what two changes they would like us to make in our own life, and then make them.

When we make needed adjustments God can use that example to bring about the needed changes in our spouse's life—including beginning to care again about the relationship.

*Dear Lord, forgive us for seeing so clearly
someone else's need to change and seeing so
poorly our own need. Amen.*

*The one who has knowledge uses words with restraint,*
*and whoever has understanding is even-tempered.*

PROVERBS 17:27

Are our words a loaded weapon?

A satirist once said, "Never miss a good opportunity to shut up." Far too often we feel compelled to say whatever is on our mind. Words can heal or they can destroy. They can energize or discourage, embolden or intimidate, and restore or repulse. That's why Scripture tells us to use words with "restraint" and to remain "even-tempered."

What words should we shun? Avoid thoughtless words—they can inflict damage you never know. Avoid sarcastic words—they'll get a laugh but at a great price. Avoid bitter words—they may leave scars for years to come. Avoid hateful words—they can kill the spirit.

If we are too upset to listen, it's a good clue we should say nothing for now. If we can't say it with kindness, we shouldn't say it at all. Finally, if we suspect we will regret what we are about to say, we probably will.

Don't miss the golden opportunity to keep quiet.

*Lord Jesus, let every word that comes from our*
*mouths this day be seasoned with salt and full*
*of grace. Amen.*

*"Therefore, if you are offering your gift at the altar
and there remember that your brother or sister
has something against you, leave your gift there
in front of the altar. First go and be reconciled
to them; then come and offer your gift."*

MATTHEW 5:23-24

Are we willing to make an apology that's truly an apology?

One of life's most difficult challenges is to admit when we're wrong, but it's a much needed virtue. In *The Five Languages of Apology*, Gary Chapman helps us to make an effective apology. First, we need to express our deep regret: "I am truly sorry." Then we should accept responsibility for our actions: "I was definitely wrong." Then we ought to make an offer of restitution: "What can I do to make this right?" Next, we should genuinely repent: "I'll not do that again." Finally, we need to request a pardon: "Will you please forgive me?"

Once we make an apology that's really an apology, wonderful things happen. First, we are restored to a right relationship with God. Second, we have opened the way to genuine reconciliation with our offended brother or sister. Finally, we go to sleep on the softest pillow of all—a clear conscience.

*Lord Jesus, give us a sense of holy urgency to
make things right with those we have offended.
Amen.*

*In your relationships with one another, have
the same mindset as Christ Jesus.*

Philippians 2:5

How can we change our attitude?

Gifted preacher Charles Swindoll once said, "The longer I live, the more I realize the impact of attitude on life…I am convinced that life is 10 percent what happens to me and 90 percent how I react to it. We are in charge of our attitudes."

Bad attitudes are usually based on the false notion of entitlement—the belief that the world owes us something. To get rid of a bad attitude requires jettisoning several things. First, we must give up our right to be number one; the world is designed to revolve around God, not us. Second, we must give up our right to be waited on; we will find life in serving, not in being served. Third, we must give up our right to use our strengths in any selfish way and use whatever gifts we possess to unselfishly love others.

Ultimately, we are called to follow the example of Jesus, who humbled Himself by becoming obedient even to death on a cross.

*Dear God, we give up our sense of entitlement
and pray our attitude will be the same as that
of Christ Jesus. Amen.*

*How sweet are your words to my taste,*
*sweeter than honey to my mouth!*
*I gain understanding from your precepts;*
*therefore I hate every wrong path.*

Psalm 119:103-104

What is more satisfying than the pleasures of sin?
John Piper, author of *Future Grace*, explains that freedom from wrongdoing begins by realizing that the promises of God are more satisfying than the gratification of sin. Though iniquity can momentarily satiate us, it can never satisfy the deepest needs of our heart. Rather, sin leaves us frustrated, ashamed, and ultimately empty.

The psalmist contrasts this unsatisfying life of transgression with the sweetness and fulfillment of obeying the Scriptures. As we delve into God's Word, we learn what true satisfaction is—learning and obeying the precepts of the Bible and hating "every wrong path." Once we see the deception of wrongdoing our natural response becomes aversion rather than indulgence.

The promises of God are a spiritual banquet that is set before us each day. The pleasures of sin are a self-imposed famine that leaves us ever wanting. Which table will we sit at?

*Lord Jesus, thank You that we can feast for*
*a lifetime on Your Word. Let it become only*
*sweeter to us as life goes on. Amen.*

*Continue to work out your salvation with fear and trembling, for it is God who works in you to will and to act in order to fulfill his good purpose.*

PHILIPPIANS 2:12-13

Should we try to change another person?

A humorist once observed that on the wedding day, the groom looks at his bride and says, "I want you to still look twenty-five when you are fifty. Please don't ever change." The bride looks at her future husband and says, "I know just how I want you to change—let's get started."

Both perspectives are wrong. God never called us to change someone, but can we have an influence in their lives? Yes, we can start by loving and accepting them unconditionally. We can praise God for the unique way He made them and be honest and patient and kind when we encounter difficulties. We can pray and fast for God to shape them in His image.

What we should never do is argue, manipulate, nag, or play substitute for the Holy Spirit. We must let God be God in their lives for He has promised to work according to His good purpose.

*Dear God, remake others in Your image and not our own. Amen.*

*"Let the little children come to me, and do not hinder them, for the kingdom of God belongs to such as these."*

LUKE 18:16

Why do our children so want our marriage to work? Parents often believe the greatest gifts they can give children are material possessions, a good education, or opportunities to excel in sports or other competitions. Yet, what children truly desire is the security of two parents who love each other. They are most at ease when the two of us are getting along well (and are most upset when they sense tension). They are most secure when we live out our promise to stay together (and struggle most when one of us is missing).

That's why the greatest gift we can give our children, second only to sharing with them our faith in Christ, is to genuinely love our spouse. Jesus said we should not hinder children from coming to Him. One way to remove such an obstacle is to remain committed and in love for a lifetime. It's a gift our children will forever treasure.

*Dear Jesus, let us have the oneness in marriage that will make it easier for our children to come to faith in You without hindrance. Amen.*

*"I have come that they may have
life, and have it to the full."*

JOHN 10:10

What difference can Jesus make in our marriage? Marriage is found among all the great religions of the world regardless of the cultural setting. What makes a Christian marriage unique among all these competing faiths? Only we Christians claim to have a living and resurrected Savior dwelling in our hearts by faith.

That produces a host of unique benefits: The Spirit of Christ empowers us to forgive each other when we don't have the strength to do so. He gives us unselfish hearts when we would otherwise demand our own way. He offers us the unlimited ability to love one another when our own love is running dry. He creates in us a deep and mysterious sense of oneness. He empowers us to resist temptation when it strikes unexpectedly. He provides direction in our daily decisions when we are confused. Finally, as we approach the end of our lives, He assures us of eternal life together.

Who else can do all that but our Jesus?

*Living Savior, thank You for giving us Your
Holy Spirit, who allows us to live our lives to
the full. Amen.*

*An honest answer is like a kiss on the lips.*

Proverbs 24:26

Will we ask our husband these honest questions? Many wives want to know how we can influence our husbands to change. Methods that have been tried and have failed are complaining, sulking, nagging, pleading, and withholding sex. If these strategies fall short when it comes to changing our mate, what might succeed?

Gary Thomas offers some surprising suggestions in his excellent book *Sacred Influence.* He proposes we ask our husband three simple questions. First, what's it like to live with my words? Wives are often more verbally skilled, so words may give us an advantage. How do you feel about that? Second, what's it like to live with my moods? Given the various swings that may occur within a month, how are they affecting you? Third, what would you change about me if you could? Are there blind spots that are creating problems for you that need to be addressed?

Just asking these three simple questions may be the beginning of your increased influence in his life—and all for the good.

*Heavenly Father, give us the trust to ask honest questions and receive honest answers like a kiss on the lips. Amen.*

*Wounds from a friend can be trusted,*
*but an enemy multiplies kisses.*

PROVERBS 27:6

When are we hurting more than helping our marriage?

There was a time in our nation's history when physicians practiced "bleeding" a patient to rid them of a disease. Unfortunately, all that was accomplished was to rid the person of his strength if not his life.

Well-intentioned as we may be, there are times when we do more harm than good in our marriage. When is this true? When we take the blame for every problem; when we believe we deserve to be mistreated; when we make excuses for our spouse's irresponsible behavior; when we pretend something doesn't matter to us but inwardly it does; when we avoid talking about vital but difficult issues; or when we are afraid to do what's right.

Love sometimes requires saying or doing some very difficult things. Scripture calls such needed words or actions the faithful "wounds from a friend." Certainly no one deserves to be loved more like a friend than your spouse.

*Dear Lord, let us never wound needlessly, but*
*only when it is required to be a faithful friend*
*to one another, and then only in love. Amen.*

*As it is written: "How beautiful are the
feet of those who bring good news!"*

ROMANS 10:15

Have you received any good news lately?

When Bob's father was serving overseas in the military, his mother would wait expectantly for his letters to arrive at her farm. She always hoped they would bring good news.

The word *gospel* literally means "good news." The gospel message begins with the fact that God loves us with an everlasting love. Though sin has separated us from God, Jesus Christ paid the penalty for our sins on the cross. By grace He offers us the free gift of eternal life in Christ Jesus. On the cross Jesus bore our guilt and sins and satisfied the justice of God. What we must do is to place our faith in the finished work of the cross and ask God for the gift of eternal life.

If you've never trusted Jesus to be your Savior and Lord, are you willing to do that today? Then the best news of your life has just arrived!

*Lord Jesus, by faith I ask You to forgive all my
sins. I place all my trust in what You
accomplished for me on the cross, and I
receive the gift of eternal life. Amen.*

*Starting a quarrel is like breaching a dam;*
*so drop the matter before a dispute breaks out.*

PROVERBS 17:14

How can we stop an argument before it gets ugly?
There's an old story about a stranger who comes upon two men on a street corner slugging it out. "Is this a private fight or can anyone join it?" he asks. Unfortunately some people seem to enjoy an altercation.

If we don't want to be such a contentious person, here are four strategies to stop an argument before it gets ugly: First, don't start one—use only helpful and beneficial words to prevent provocation. Second, don't join one—offer only gentle and respectful responses in the face of hostile and aggressive words. Third, don't internalize one—choose not to take it personally when an offensive word is spoken. Fourth, don't continue one—once a disagreement is resolved, don't go back and revisit it again and again.

Scripture says starting a quarrel is like breaching a dam, so drop the matter before a dispute breaks out.

*Lord Jesus, help us to remember it's impossible*
*to speak in a whisper and argue for very long.*
*Amen.*

*Enter his gates with thanksgiving
and his courts with praise;
give thanks to him and praise his name.*

PSALM 100:4

Can we visit God's temple each day?

The beginning of each day is an opportunity to enter the gates of the Lord. No, we don't have to attend church or visit a cathedral, but simply bow in prayer and we are immediately ushered inside His temple. The Bible says the proper way to go through the door is with praise and thanksgiving. If we do so, it will yield numerous spiritual blessings: It will allow God to give us an entirely new perspective on the day's problems and challenges. It will help us see how big God truly is and how small our problems truly are. It will allow us to value what God truly values. It will permit us to see that knowing Jesus Christ is infinitely more valuable than all the world's treasures. And it will open the way for God to work miracles in our life.

Praise and thanksgiving are an invitation into the very throne room of Almighty God. Will we respond to it?

*Heavenly Father, before we leave our house,
may we visit Yours. Amen.*

*Finally, all of you, be like-minded, be sympathetic,
love one another, be compassionate and humble.*

1 Peter 3:8

How should we respond to our wife's emotions? George Kenworthy's insightful book, *Marriage Makeover,* offers help in understanding and responding properly to our wife's emotions. Don't tell her she's acting too emotional or being too sensitive—simply because she has a different emotional makeup doesn't mean she's wrong and we're right. Don't become impatient if she can't explain why she's feeling the way she does—there is a mystery and complexity to the female heart that should be celebrated rather than judged. Listen and pray for increased sensitivity to her heart and give her a strong shoulder on which to lean, cry, laugh, and love. It is a sign of masculine strength to respond in gentleness and sensitivity to the emotional pendulum a wife can sometimes experience. Finally, imitate the understanding Jesus displayed to the woman who poured perfume on His feet. While others were ready to criticize, Jesus saw her true motivations and praised her for it.

*Lord Jesus, let harmony, sympathy, love,
compassion, and humility control our response
to one another—different as we are. Amen.*

*Jesus replied, "Moses permitted you to divorce
your wives because your hearts were hard. But
it was not this way from the beginning."*

MATTHEW 19:8

Have we hardened our heart toward our mate?

Smart drivers take warning signs, such as flashing lights in a construction zone, seriously. We should do the same when our hearts indicate a clear and present danger sign that we are hardening our heart toward our spouse. A hard heart is simply a settled attitude of rejection toward our mate, and Jesus said it's ultimately the cause of all divorce.

What are some of the warning signs we should heed? Constant sarcasm and criticism are an indication that we are carrying hidden anger in our heart. Emotional window-shopping is another warning signal. That's when we begin looking at other individuals and wonder if they would make a better mate than our own. Leveraging our love by withholding it until our spouse gives in is yet one more sign.

The only certain cure for our hard heart is to confess our attitude as sin, seek God's forgiveness, and ask Christ to replace it with His tender heart.

*Lord Jesus, help us to recognize the warning
signs of a hard heart and to change course
before it's too late. Amen.*

*Now I want you to know, brothers and sisters, that what has happened to me has actually served to advance the gospel.*

Philippians 1:12

How do we handle unexpected trouble?

The world seems to be divided between those who look for a way *out* of trouble and those who look for a way *through* it. In Jay Adams's helpful little booklet, *How to Handle Trouble,* he offers practical biblical advice on how to successfully work through life's unexpected difficulties.

First we must recognize God is in our problem and has promised to never leave or forsake us. Next, we must believe God is always up to something good and that He never wastes our pain or difficulties. Then we should look for how and where God is at work. Regardless of how hopeless things may seem, we can always find evidence of God bringing a greater good in our troubles. Finally, we need to get involved in what God is doing. Rather than resist God, we need to cooperate and expect a good result.

If we follow this advice, we will be able to victoriously say, like Paul, "What has happened to me has actually served to advance the gospel."

*Dear Jesus, may You show us the way through our troubles this day. Amen.*

*The LORD said to me, "Go, show your love
to your wife again, though she is loved by
another man and is an adulteress."*

HOSEA 3:1

Can there be forgiveness for an affair?

No deeper wound occurs in a marriage than when one partner cheats on the other. The only chance for saving the marriage is through genuine repentance and forgiveness. Repentance is saying, "I will never do it again," and meaning it. Forgiveness is releasing another person from the moral debt they owe us. We must forgive just as God in Christ forgave us of all our sins.

Some may argue, "But if I forgive isn't that just setting myself up for another possible devastating experience?" That's where it's vital to recognize the difference between forgiveness and reconciliation. Forgiveness is required of us regardless of the offense. But reconciliation occurs only if the offending person acknowledges their sin, shows genuine remorse, offers a heartfelt apology, pledges not to repeat the sin, and makes a good-faith effort to restore what they have ruined.

Forgiveness is possible in any situation, and with God's help, so is reconciliation.

*Heavenly Father, regardless of the sins, may
we extend that same grace we have received
to those who have deeply wounded our hearts.
Amen.*

*For our struggle is not against flesh and blood, but*
*against the rulers, against the authorities, against*
*the powers of this dark world and against the*
*spiritual forces of evil in the heavenly realms.*

EPHESIANS 6:12

How can we win against the spiritual forces of evil?
If we could obtain a spiritual Doppler-radar image of the earth, we would see massive thunderheads of wickedness swirling about—what the Bible calls spiritual forces of evil in the heavenly realms. How can we mortals possibly be victorious over such massive dark powers?

Scripture tells us we are to stand in the authority of Christ's name. At the cross, Jesus defeated and took captive all the hosts of darkness. That means that every foe we face is a defeated foe. The mighty Lion of Judah, Jesus Christ, has faced down all the powers of hell and prevailed. Now, as His followers, we can pray and claim His authority and victory, and the forces of darkness must flee.

*Lord Jesus, thank You that on the cross You*
*defeated and took captive all the forces of evil.*
*May we stand in Your name and authority*
*and resist all evil to find victory. Amen.*

*God was reconciling the world to himself in*
*Christ, not counting people's sins against them.*

2 Corinthians 5:19

How can we wipe our record clean? Financial counselors advise couples it takes at least seven years to expunge a negative report on our credit score. It takes time to prove we deserve a clean record. What can we do to remove from our spiritual credit score the mistakes, wrongs, and sins of our past? Does it require that we change our behavior, avoid making similar errors, and over time prove we are worthy to receive God's favor?

Thankfully, God has provided a better way to forever scrub our record of all the negative reports. The Bible tells us God was reconciling us to Himself in Christ "not counting people's sins against them." The reason God is able to wipe our account clean is that Jesus bore all of our sinful offenses and transferred them to His file. At the cross, all our sins were forever expunged by the precious blood of the Lord Jesus.

Doesn't getting a clean record sound good?

*Heavenly Father, thank You that You no longer*
*count our sins but have by grace declared us free*
*and clear, now and forever. Amen.*

*When the storm has swept by, the wicked are gone,*
*but the righteous stand firm forever.*

PROVERBS 10:25

Can our marriage relationship survive a hurricane?
The aftermath of a storm demonstrates the true structural strength or weakness of a building. The same is true of our marriage. When the winds of financial loss, career setbacks, health problems, and prodigal children have swept by, we discover just how strong or how tottering our relationship truly is. Some couples emerge from their tempests with their love and intimacy for each other in ruins while other couples are more deeply committed than ever.

The key to surviving gale force winds in life is personal righteousness, according to Scripture. If we remain rightly related to God, dependent upon His Word and living our lives in the power of the Holy Spirit, we are promised "the righteous stand firm forever." None of us can prevent storms from sweeping into our lives, nor can we control their intensity or duration. Yet, we do have control over our response and can choose to live in a right and close relationship with Jesus.

*Lord Jesus, You said to the storm, "Quiet! Be*
*still!" and all was silent. Thank You that You*
*are Lord of the storm. Amen.*

*Therefore, since we are surrounded by such a great*
*cloud of witnesses, let us throw off everything that*
*hinders and the sin that so easily entangles.*

HEBREWS 12:1

Do we need someone to cheer us on today?
Most of us know dear people who have gone
before us to heaven. Perhaps it was our loving father or
mother, a godly pastor, or a close friend who impacted
our life with their strong faith and caring heart. The Bible
tells us they now stand in the presence of God. Though
no longer with us, their righteous examples can continue
to serve as a "great cloud of witnesses" surrounding us in
our here and now.

Can't we almost see them cheering us on from the
grandstands of heaven? Can't we almost hear them urging us onward to pursue God's kingdom? Can't we almost
imagine them smiling and nodding as they watch us fight
the good fight of faith?

May their example serve as an incentive for us to
"throw off everything that hinders." As we consider the
outcome of their faith, we can resist sin and temptation.
Best of all, someday they will be there to welcome us home
across the great finish line.

*Lord Jesus, keep our eyes fixed on You,*
*the Pioneer and Perfecter of our faith. Amen.*

*Houses and wealth are inherited from parents,*
*but a prudent wife is from the LORD.*

PROVERBS 19:14

What five gifts will our wife never forget?

We husbands can sometimes struggle trying to find just the right present for our spouse for birthdays, anniversaries, or Christmas. Look no further, because there are five gifts that we can choose from (we recommend giving them all) that she will cherish forever. No, they don't involve expensive diamonds or flowers or a new car. Rather, they all involve giving the gift(s) of ourselves.

Why not present her with the Gift of Unhurried Time Together, the Gift of Undivided Attention, the Gift of Unconditional Love, the Gift of Acts of Kindness, and the Gift of Unsolicited Praise. Each of these valuable presents is free, yet they all will cost us something to present to her. What gift is of value that doesn't involve sacrifice?

Thankfully these gifts are appropriate for any season of the year and go well with anything she owns. Proverbs tells us to show extravagant generosity to our wife, because it is God who gave her to us as His present.

*Dear God, You are the true gift giver—You*
*gave us Yourself in the Lord Jesus. Amen.*

*Now when Jesus saw the crowds, he went
up on a mountainside and sat down. His
disciples came to him, and he began to teach
them. He said: "Blessed are the..."*

Matthew 5:1-3

Does our life reflect the Beautiful Attitudes?
Many people spend their lives pursuing happiness,
yet never seem to find it. It is likely they are looking for it
in all the wrong places. The biblical word for *happiness* is
often translated "blessed" and is used repeatedly by Jesus
in His Sermon on the Mount.

What some would call the Beatitudes we call the Beautiful Attitudes. We reflect a beautiful attitude when we:
admit that without God we really have nothing in life;
are willing to mourn over our sins; display a humble attitude in all of life; seek to live, think, and act rightly toward
each other; show mercy toward someone in need of mercy;
don't entertain impure thoughts; are the first to seek peace
in our relationship when it is interrupted; and agree to follow Jesus no matter the cost.

All these beautiful attitudes will result in God's lasting
blessing and ultimately—surprise—happiness.

*Our Lord Jesus, thank You that true happiness
is found in a life of blessed attitudes. Amen.*

*We demolish arguments and every pretension that sets
itself up against the knowledge of God, and we take
captive every thought to make it obedient to Christ.*

2 Corinthians 10:5

Can our thoughts take us hostage?

Shakespeare wrote, "Make not your thoughts your prison." We can become captives to our own thinking, particularly when that thinking is in error. That's why couples often repeat the same old arguments over and over. Or continue the same non-productive pattern of speaking before listening. Or pursue the same flawed goal of trying to change the other person.

The Bible tells us we are to "take captive every thought to make it obedient to Christ." What does that look like in practice? It requires us to make a comparison between our thoughts and the truths of Scripture. For example, if we are caught in the rut of thinking our spouse is the one with all the problems, we are challenged by Romans 3:23, "for all have sinned and fall short of the glory of God."

Once we choose God's truth over a lie we have believed, our thinking changes and a prisoner goes free.

*Heavenly Father, thank You that it was for
freedom we have been set free, including from
wrong thinking. Amen.*

*But the angel said to them, "Do not be*
*afraid. I bring you good news that will*
*cause great joy for all the people."*

LUKE 2:10

What is the essence of joy?

That first Christmas night the angels told a group of trembling shepherds they had cause for great joy. Why? The Lord Jesus had entered the world to redeem us from our sins.

Today that same good news should bring about a profound change in our priorities. As children we were taught that J-O-Y means, "Jesus first, Others second, You last." Jesus must come first for us to know true joy—nothing fits into place unless Jesus gets top priority. "Others second" is based on the profound truth it is more blessed to give than receive. Joy enters our lives as we discover the honor and fulfillment of blessing others. "You last" refers to our need to abandon self-focus and discover the true humility of Christ. Paul writes, "In your relationships with one another, have the same mindset as Christ Jesus who… made himself nothing" (Philippians 2:5,7).

When we put Christ first, others second, and ourselves last, we discover the essence of true and lasting joy.

*Dear Lord Jesus, thank You that You are the*
*joy and strength of our lives. Amen.*

## — DAY 161 —

*Didn't the* L*ORD* *make you one with your wife? In body and spirit you are his.*

MALACHI 2:15 NLT

How married are you?

We sometimes encounter married couples who seem to be living separate lives. They maintain different bank accounts, take independent vacations, and may even have separate groups of friends. Yet they often lament that their marriage is stale and unfulfilling. The problem is while they are legally married, they are living as if they were single.

Here's a quick test to determine how married we are. Level One is an *armed truce* marked by subdued but ongoing hostility. Level Two is *bored roommates* characterized by apathy and aloofness. Level Three is *good business partners* marked by utility and functional organizational roles. Level Four is *good friends* characterized by cordiality and limited access. Level Five is *committed and growing lovers* demonstrated by transparency and investment in the relationship. And Level Six is *intimate soul mates* evidenced by vulnerability and giving and receiving love freely.

If your relationship is somewhere between Level One and Level Four, may we make a suggestion? Why not get really married?

*Our heavenly Father, thank You for designing us to be one. May we settle for nothing less in our marriage. Amen.*

*A hot-tempered person stirs up conflict,*
*but the one who is patient calms a quarrel.*

PROVERBS 15:18

What is a marital anger contract?

As adults we enter into a number of important legal agreements. We sign a home mortgage or a rental agreement. We may put our signature on a new car purchase or a three-year lease. We may even put our initials on a multi-year mobile phone deal. Yet, we may have never entered into one of marriage's most important contracts.

David and Claudia Arp, in their insightful book *The Second Half of Marriage*, believe each couple should formulate an anger contract containing three promises: First, we will acknowledge our anger to the other person as soon as we become aware of it. Second, we will not attack the other person, nor will we defend ourselves. Finally, we will ask for the other person's help in dealing with the anger that has developed. The goal is to have a predetermined relationship covenant on how you will handle anger—one of life's most potentially destructive emotions.

It's sound advice and a helpful way to contract love.

*Our Savior, may we walk together in*
*agreement throughout our marriage. Amen.*

*A brother wronged is more unyielding*
*than a fortified city;*
*disputes are like the barred gates of a citadel.*

PROVERBS 18:19

W hy is it foolish to stay angry?
While it's a temptation of our fallen nature to stay upset once we've been offended, it really is counterproductive to loving relationships. There are several reasons why letting go of our negative emotions as quickly as possible makes sense.

To begin with, time spent in bitterness and isolation is time forever wasted. While we can often recover money, property, or even a lost reputation, we can never reclaim time once lost. Furthermore, the longer a wound remains open, the deeper the scar. Unresolved emotions have a way of festering as time goes on. A barrier of sin with my spouse creates a barrier with God as bitterness creates both horizontal and vertical walls. Finally, our children pay the biggest price when we spouses remain angry. Their tender hearts are confused, discouraged, and frightened by their parents deeply at odds with each other.

Little if anything is to be gained by remaining angry at one another, except heartache for all concerned.

*Lord Jesus, may the Holy Spirit remind us*
*each day that love keeps no record of wrongs.*
*Amen.*

*And he will be called
Wonderful Counselor, Mighty God,
Everlasting Father, Prince of Peace.*

Isaiah 9:6

Can Christmas bring healing to our life?

While the Christmas season is a time of joy and celebration for many families, for others it only adds more stress and strain. Thankfully, the birth of Christ as foretold in Isaiah holds four promises for healing and relief for hurting relationships.

First, we can trust Jesus to give us the advice we need—He is the Wonderful Counselor. There is no problem too perplexing for Him to solve. Second, Jesus can give us the power to overcome any problem we are facing—He is the Mighty God. Our relationship mountains are "just a hill from heaven's point of view." Next, Jesus offers us the unconditional love and acceptance we long for—He is the Everlasting Father. He welcomes us into His caring arms regardless of what we or someone else has done. Finally, Jesus can bring calm to our relationships—He is the Prince of Peace. He can bring needed reconciliation where estrangement has existed far too long.

As the Christmas hymn reminds us, Jesus will bring us "healing in His wings."

*Precious Savior, let the joy You brought to
the world at Your birth find its way into our
hearts. Amen.*

*And I pray that you, being rooted and established
in love, may have power, together with all
the Lord's holy people, to grasp how wide and
long and high and deep is the love of Christ.*

EPHESIANS 3:17-18

Is there any shortage of God's love?

Love is God's ultimately renewable resource. That same endless source of love can renew our marriage. However it requires taking these four steps. First, we choose to spend the rest of our life with our spouse. Love results from the choices we make, not the feelings we achieve. Second, we choose to make our marriage the first priority in our life after our relationship with Christ. The more we value our mate, the more love will flow from our heart. Third, we choose to act in love to again feel in love. As we behave in a loving fashion, it transforms our emotions. Finally, we choose to believe God has a wonderful plan for our marriage.

Faith in God's good purposes and lordship open the doors for His love to be shed abroad in our marriage relationship.

*Dear Jesus, Your love is deeper than the ocean
and higher than the heavens. Let that
boundless love be released in our hearts. Amen.*

*How beautiful you are, my darling!*
*Oh, how beautiful! Your eyes are doves.*

Song of Songs 1:15

What is our mate's love language?

Gary Chapman has done us a great service by identifying five basic love languages. A love language is the particular way we prefer to express and receive love. We both feel loved when we learn to speak and act upon each other's love language.

The first love language is *physical touch*—this person needs physical contact to experience love. The second is *quality time*—spending long and uninterrupted periods together reaches their heart. The third love language is *gifts*—giving simple presents communicates that we are thinking of them, and they feel important. The fourth is *acts of service*—we perform tasks that make our spouse's life easier, and they feel cherished. The fifth love language is *words of affirmation*—these are genuine compliments we offer, leaving them basking in assurance they are valued.

Learning each other's love language can become the turning point in our marriage. Isn't it time we took the time and effort to become fluent in our mate's special love language?

*Heavenly Father, thank You that You speak*
*our love language in the person of Jesus. Amen.*

*For the lips of the adulteress woman drip honey,*
*and her speech is smoother than oil;*
*but in the end she is bitter as gall,*
*sharp as a double-edged sword.*

PROVERBS 5:3-4

What are five ways to guard faithfulness in marriage? While sexual temptation can exert a powerful attraction, the truths of Scripture can counteract its magnetism. Here are five specific truths to guard us from making one of life's worst decisions.

First, adultery appears sweet to begin with, but it quickly turns bitter and painful. Second, adultery is an act of pure selfishness and not real love. True love would never compromise a vow in order to fulfill one's desires. Third, adultery exchanges one set of problems for another usually far worse. Whatever our present difficulties, the consequences of adultery will make them pale in comparison. Fourth, adultery is trading in a faithful partner for a betrayer; a person willing to commit adultery is not worthy of us. Fifth, adultery damages the lives of innocent people forever. No mate deserves the ongoing anguish of infidelity, nor do our children merit the lifelong heart damage it will cause.

*Dear God, keep us as faithful to one another*
*as Christ is true to His church. Amen.*

*"Love your neighbor as yourself." If you
bite and devour each other, watch out or
you will be destroyed by each other.*

Galatians 5:14-15

Who is seated on the throne of our life today?

The great evangelist Bill Bright explains the battle between our fallen nature and our new nature as a throne room in our hearts. There either Jesus Christ, the rightful King, sits upon the throne of our lives, or our sinful self, the great usurper, takes control.

This analogy can help explain why we can argue, bicker, and attack one another. It clarifies why we battle for control rather than pursuing self-control. It makes clear why we allow resentment rather than peace to grow up. It sheds light on why we have a greater desire to be right than to be a loving person.

Once we realize that self and not the Lord Jesus is on the throne, we can work to resolve our conflict. We need to quickly confess our sin to God, ask for His forgiveness, and then invite Jesus to take His rightful place on the throne of our life once again.

*Lord Jesus, You alone have the right to the
throne of our lives this day. Amen.*

*Honor her for all that her hands have done,*
*and let her works bring her praise at the city gate.*

PROVERBS 31:31

What do we wives wish our husbands understood? Wives can carry important but unexpressed feelings they long for their husbands to know about. We feel responsible for everyone. Given our natural tendencies to nurture, we can try to take care of everyone all the time, and we need your encouragement to practice self-care. When you criticize us, it carries incredible weight. We put far more stock and meaning in words than you realize, so please choose words carefully. We measure success by our relationships and not our achievements. We need your time and attention to feel loved. We can enjoy making love only when we feel close to you. It helps when you are willing to resolve the tensions in our relationship before suggesting we be intimate. Finally, it's easy for us to think you are upset with us even if you aren't. Please offer us the reassurance all is well so we don't have to guess.

*Lord Jesus, help us to live with one another*
*according to knowledge and not assumptions.*
*Amen.*

*The purposes of a person's heart are deep waters,*
*But one who has insight draws them out.*

Proverbs 20:5

What are some secrets of the male heart?

We husbands are not always comfortable sharing our feelings and struggles, but here are things we wish our wife knew: When we are quiet, we are probably dealing with stress or pain; we are not deliberately trying to ignore you. When things go bad at work, we can feel like failures; it really helps to have you express confidence in us. When confronted with intense emotions like crying, we don't quite know how to respond; please reassure us it will pass and you'll be okay. When we feel disrespected, we feel unloved; it's hard to explain why, but just accept that showing us honor is the way we feel loved. Even when we fail to say "I love you," we do still love you; we prefer to show it in nonverbal ways, such as providing, protecting, and remaining faithful.

These secrets are now no longer secrets are they?

*Dear Jesus, help us draw out the purposes of*
*each other's heart that we might honor and*
*love one another. Amen.*

*"For where your treasure is, there
your heart will be also."*

MATTHEW 6:21

Is our wealth in this world or the next?

It's easy to become focused on the temporary values of life rather than on eternity. These temporal values can take a particularly heavy toll on our relationships when our pursuit of personal goals leaves our spouse feeling neglected, unloved, and alone. Giving all to our career can cause our children to feel overlooked or even abandoned. As the disconnection grows at home, our tendency is to invest even more at work. Sadly, that can lead to emotional or physical involvement with a coworker, setting up the final dissolution of our marriage.

God made us for eternal values, not temporary ones. If we are caught up in temporal values, let's call it what it is—sin. We should repent and refocus from building treasures on earth to storing true wealth in heaven. Careers, money, and pleasure can never substitute for an intimate relationship with God, our spouse, and our children. Only eternal values can satisfy.

*Heavenly Father, may we make deposits of love,
faithfulness, and sacrifice each day
in the bank of heaven, where they will
remain forever. Amen.*

*But if we walk in the light, as he is in the
light, we have fellowship with one another.*

1 JOHN 1:7

Is it time to take off a mask?

Hypocrisy is pretending to be something on the outside we are not on the inside. In classical Greek, the term meant literally "to wear a mask," referring to costume masks worn by actors on stage.

The masks we wear can take several forms in marriage, according to one marriage counselor. A husband who is living in moral failure can pretend to be living an upright life—that's hypocrisy. A wife can be secretly fantasizing about men she believes would be more caring, yet she pretends to be faithful—that's hypocrisy. A couple that is constantly bickering at home can present to the outside world a picture of a harmonious marriage—but that's hypocrisy.

To restore emotional intimacy we need to confess our hypocrisy to God and ask Him to remove our mask. Such confession, repentance, honesty, and transparency will restore genuine emotional intimacy and caring to a marriage.

*Lord Jesus, give us the courage and character
to be the same people in private and public
and thus bless our marriage with
true authenticity. Amen.*

*For God was pleased…to reconcile to himself all*
*things, whether things on earth or things in heaven,*
*by making peace through his blood, shed on the cross.*

Colossians 1:19-20

Where can we take our bitterness and disappointment?

Most of us have experienced the pain of being treated poorly or unjustly. When confronted with such pain and disappointment, we are left with only three choices: we can turn it inward, outward, or upward. If we turn it inward, we will allow our hurt, pain, frustration, and anger to eventually morph into depression. If we turn it outward, we will unfairly take out our hurt and frustration on those closest to us in anger and aggression. If we turn it upward, we will take it to the cross of Jesus Christ in humility and surrender. It is there that Christ took upon Himself all our desire for revenge, retribution, or hate that we might carry.

Nothing has happened to us that didn't happen to Jesus in one form or another. He understands our wounded hearts and knows how to set us free. Let's take our bitterness and disappointment to the cross right now—and leave it there.

*Lord Jesus, thank You that on the cross You*
*reconciled all things in heaven and on earth*
*through Your blood. Amen.*

*For God so loved the world that he gave his
one and only Son, that whoever believes in
him shall not perish but have eternal life.*

JOHN 3:16

What if we are feeling unloved at the moment?
While marriage can be a wonderfully fulfilling
relationship, it was never designed to meet all our needs—
only Jesus can do that. If we are not feeling as loved as we
wish, we need not despair. The Bible tells us God loves us
with an everlasting love. It was dramatically demonstrated
in the sacrifice of God's one and only Son for our sins.
When we are tempted to feel unappreciated or unloved,
we need to remember the boundless love of God for us.

To fully experience this amazing love, the Bible tells us
we must believe in the Lord Jesus Christ. Have you taken
that step of faith yet? If not, we encourage you right now
to place your complete trust in the finished work of Christ
on the cross on your behalf. With such a new life comes
God's promise of deep, continual, undying love and eternal life that will be yours now and forever—and the reassuring knowledge we are never alone.

*Lord Jesus, we choose to believe and therefore
know that we shall not perish but have
everlasting life. Amen.*

*For it is by grace you have been saved, through faith—and this is not from yourselves, it is the gift of God—not by works, so that no one can boast.*

EPHESIANS 2:8-9

Are we still trying to earn God's love?

Imagine going to a birthday party where the guest of honor walks around the circle of friends and offers each person a wad of cash to cover the price of the gift they just gave. Ridiculous? Of course. Once we pay for a gift, it's no longer a gift; it's simply a business transaction.

If we were raised in a home where love was conditional and forgiveness was earned, we may find it difficult to accept the unconditional love of our husband or wife. Furthermore, we may struggle to believe God accepts us, and if He does, it's only because we've earned His favor.

It's time for us to reject all such wrong thinking and stop all efforts to deserve God's love. For love to truly be love, it must be free, unconditional, and truly a gift. Today is the day to unwrap the present of God's love and grace and simply say, "Thank you."

*Lord Jesus, no amount of work or effort would ever pay for the love You have freely given us. Amen.*

*But God demonstrates his own love for us in this:*
*While we were still sinners, Christ died for us.*

ROMANS 5:8

Is true love based on commitment or feelings?

A university study discovered the dreamy feelings of infatuation are produced by hormones that wear out in two to three years. That's when many couples conclude they have lost their love for each other. They may even assume the marriage is over because sensations of romance are gone.

Yet true love is never built on the shifting sands of feelings alone. It's constructed on the rock-solid commitment to lifelong fidelity. Choosing to unselfishly focus on our spouse's needs won't always produce warm sensations of romance, but it's the stuff of genuine love. The Bible says God demonstrated His love for us in that while we were yet sinners, Christ died for us. God made a commitment to love the human race even when we were anything but lovely and attractive.

Feelings of love are marvelous, but they can come and go. Committed love abides through all the seasons of life—and in the end is far more satisfying.

*Lord Jesus, thank You that Your love for us is*
*not shifting or temporary but constant and*
*abiding. Amen.*

*Then the LORD said to Cain, "Why are you angry? Why is your face downcast? If you do what is right, will you not be accepted?"*

GENESIS 4:6-7

What's the true cause of anger?

The nineteenth-century explorer and missionary David Livingston set out to find the source of the Nile River. He came close but never actually located the headwaters. Have you tried to explore the real source of the negative emotions that impact your marriage? We could blame our unhealthy anger on our spouse. Or we can assign its cause to our natural temperament or cultural upbringing. While close, they are not the real source.

Interestingly, the first time the word *anger* appears in the Bible, it's in relation to two brothers. The Lord warns Cain that the real source of his anger is not his brother Abel, but that he is out of right relationship with God.

If we are sinfully angry, we need to examine our hearts to locate where we strayed in our relationship with God. Then we need to go back and repent of our wrongdoing. God promises if we do what is right, we will be accepted and our anger will disappear.

*Lord Jesus, use my unhealthy anger as a map to point me back to the place where I left Your path. Amen.*

*Even when I am old and gray,*
*do not forsake me, my God,*
*till I declare your power to the next generation,*
*your mighty acts to all who are to come.*

PSALM 71:18

Have we applied the nursing home test to our priorities?

When we begin our married lives, the pressure is strong to start our career, buy a home, and provide financial security for our new family. Yet as time goes by, we can find ourselves neglecting the more important matter of our relationships. Children are born, grow up, and soon are gone. If we're not careful, we will have wasted precious years on lesser pursuits.

How can we avoid making such a tragic mistake? We suggest using the nursing home test. Should we live to be quite elderly and confined to a nursing home, who will come see us? Or remind us of our name? Or feed us supper? It will likely be our spouse or children or grandchildren—not our employer, neighbor, or stockbroker.

Why not invest today in the relationships that will last for all of life—and then on into eternity?

*Lord, help us remember that our days are*
*fleeting and that relationships are life's most*
*precious gifts. Amen.*

*"Consider how far you have fallen! Repent
and do the things you did at first."*

REVELATION 2:5

How can we feel in love again?

An older couple was riding together in a car when the wife looked wistfully at her husband and said, "Remember when I used to sit next to you?" Without batting an eye, the husband replied, "I'm not the one who moved."

Jesus told the church in Ephesus they should, "Repent and do the things you did at first." That advice can apply to restoring love in our marriage as well. We don't need an exotic vacation or new vitamin supplement or customized exercise regimen to act lovingly toward one another again. We simply need to recall when we first met. Didn't we hold hands in the restaurant? Didn't we write each other thoughtful notes? Didn't we spend time talking on the phone about our day?

Feelings of romance are rekindled when we start doing the loving and thoughtful things we did at first. Don't wait for feelings to act romantic; act romantic and watch the feelings flame up again.

*Lord Jesus, forgive us for letting time and
busyness extinguish the loving behaviors and
caring gestures of our early days. Amen.*

*Above all else, guard your heart,*
*for everything you do flows from it.*

PROVERBS 4:23

What does it mean to guard our heart?

It's becoming more common to purchase home security systems that allow us to monitor our homes while we are away. As important as it is to guard our possessions in real time, it's far more vital we guard our heart moment by moment.

Nancy Leigh DeMoss and Tim Grissom, two insightful authors, share seven practical strategies to use to protect our hearts against sin invasion: (1) recognize our real potential to sin; (2) realize that as believers we don't have to give in to sin; (3) resolve ahead of time to live a pure and godly life; (4) remove all forms of bitterness from our lives; (5) run from every form of evil; (6) renew our mind with the Word of God; and (7) refuse to remain in defeat and depression.

Victories of the heart are more often won in the preparation than in the actual battle. Scripture reminds us above all else to guard our heart—it is the wellspring of life.

*Heavenly Father, prepare us daily to protect*
*the most precious item You have created in*
*us—our heart. Amen.*

*"At the resurrection people will neither
marry nor be given in marriage; they
will be like the angels in heaven."*

Matthew 22:30

Why won't there be marriage in heaven?
Some couples secretly lament the idea there will
be no marriage in eternity. They are tempted to believe
heaven, at least in this respect, will be less satisfying than
earth was. Yet, God has promised that the new heaven and
new earth will be infinitely more satisfying, fulfilling, and
enjoyable than anything this life offered.

The reason there's no marriage in eternity is that all
the purposeful lessons marriage taught us on earth about
the relationship between Christ and the church will be
fulfilled. As the bride of Christ, we will now be forever
present with the bridegroom, Jesus. We'll experience trust,
intimacy, loyalty, friendship, fidelity, kindness, and acceptance on a level far greater than our experience of marriage on earth.

At the same time, there's little doubt we'll be able to
recognize, fellowship with, and show love to our life's mate
(assuming they are a believer in Christ). But our true and
lasting marriage will be to Jesus Christ forever.

*Lord Jesus, thank You that one day as believers
we shall be seated with honor at the wedding
supper of the Lamb. Amen.*

*The end of a matter is better than its beginning,*
*and patience is better than pride.*

ECCLESIASTES 7:8

Why is growing old together so worthwhile?
In a culture obsessed with staying forever young,
the idea of aging together doesn't seem all that attractive.
Yet, God designed marriage so that the end of our days
together can be far better than the beginning. By then
we should have come to accept each other with all our
unique strengths and weaknesses. Though in the early
years we might have attempted to change each other, we
now understand that mutual acceptance is a much more
satisfying experience.

We may have watched our children grow from infancy
into adulthood and take spouses of their own. We likely
made wonderful friends along the way who have grown
only more precious. Hopefully time has deepened our
character and solidified our faith as we faced and survived
difficult storms together.

Yes, aging has its distinct challenges, but the key is to
continue to grow together not apart. With the promise of
heaven, we can be assured the best is yet to come.

*Our Lord Jesus, grant us the gift of growing old*
*together that we might treasure one another all*
*the days of our life. Amen.*

*I have fought the good fight, I have finished*
*the race, I have kept the faith.*

2 TIMOTHY 4:7

How can we finish life together with no regrets? Four words capture the essence of regret, "What could have been…" Yet, we need not finish life lamenting. We can resolve starting today to say only loving things to each other so there will be no more words to take back. We can make time now for our children, remembering they will never be younger than they are today. We can begin giving more to others instead of taking so that we'll never end up feeling sorry for ourselves. We can today express real and sincere appreciation for our spouse and continue to keep all the promises we made to them.

Most important, we can make Christ the center of our marriage and give our lives in the service of the King. We'll then experience the joy of a life well-lived with eternal rewards. If we begin doing these things this very day, at the end of our life we'll be able to honestly say, "We have no regrets."

*Heavenly Father, may the only thing we regret*
*at life's end is how short it was together. Amen.*

*May the grace of the Lord Jesus Christ, and*
*the love of God, and the fellowship of*
*the Holy Spirit be with you all.*

2 Corinthians 13:14

What can the Trinity teach us about marriage? Where does the design for marriage come from? Is it simply a useful social construct as some sociologists argue? Is it the product only of evolutionary advantages as some anthropologists believe? Or are its real origins found in something far more glorious and mysterious?

Scripture teaches that the blueprint of marriage has its origins in the Holy Trinity, the one Godhead composed of three distinct persons—Father, Son, and Holy Spirit. Consider that throughout Scripture, perfect harmony, trust, and love exist within the Trinity. Each Person perfectly complements the role of the other. Each Member fulfills His duty with joy, completion, and confidence. There is unfailing love, support, and communication within the Godhead.

When God declared that He would make mankind "in our image," He was saying, among other things, we were created to know the indescribable fulfillment and deep love that exists between the Father, Son, and Holy Spirit.

*O great Godhead, grant us a marriage that*
*mirrors the love, unity, and trust of the divine*
*Trinity. Amen.*

*We were under great pressure, far beyond our*
*ability to endure, so that we despaired of life*
*itself...But this happened that we might not rely*
*on ourselves but on God, who raises the dead.*

2 CORINTHIANS 1:8-9

What can we do when we're ready to call it quits?
An old cliché teaches when we reach the end of our rope, we should tie a knot and hang on. The apostle Paul reached a point where he "despaired of life" and felt under "the sentence of death." Yet it was at this very breaking-point that he experienced a life-changing lesson—we should rely on God and not on ourselves.

When we are most ready to call it quits, throw in the towel, and run up the white flag, the power of God is most available to us. It's only when we run out of answers and options that we discover the true faithfulness of God. If things are at a nadir point in our life or marriage today, take heart—this may be to teach us to rely on God and not ourselves.

Perhaps that's one reason they call getting married "tying the knot."

*Dear Jesus, may Your strength be made perfect*
*in our weaknesses. Amen.*

*What is more, I consider everything a loss because*
*of the surpassing worth of knowing Christ Jesus*
*my Lord, for whose sake I have lost all things.*

PHILIPPIANS 3:8

What good can come out of aging?

Someone has said the process of growing older is learning to manage our losses. Our children grow up, our time with our mate grows shorter by the day, and our health begins to decline. Every married couple that stays together for a lifetime can expect to cope with these difficulties and more as time go on.

Paul taught that regardless of what we lose as life goes by, it pales in comparison to "the surpassing worth of knowing Christ Jesus my Lord." For in knowing Jesus Christ, we have the promise of the restoration of all things upon His return. The day is coming when Christ shall descend from heaven and all that we have lost in life shall be restored, only now in a glorified form—and that includes these mortal bodies.

*Lord Jesus, allow us to surrender gracefully all*
*the things of this world until all we have left is*
*You. For You are going to bring about the*
*restoration of all things. Amen.*

*I have learned the secret of being content in*
*any and every situation, whether well fed or*
*hungry, whether living in plenty or in want.*

PHILIPPIANS 4:12

What's required to experience true contentment? What would it take for us to feel satisfied? A new job? A new house? A new mate? All of the above? Unfortunately far too many married couples go through life discontented with their spouse, economic status, the neighborhood they live in, and the list goes on. The Bible says that's so unnecessary.

The apostle Paul claimed to have learned the "secret of being content in any and every situation." He didn't find it through visualization or meditation techniques, or through an expanded line of credit, or by picking the right numbers and hitting the lottery jackpot. What was the essence of his discovery? "I can do all this through him who gives me strength." It was Paul's moment by moment reliance on the strength that the indwelling Christ gave him that enabled him to face each day with true peace, thankfulness, and satisfaction.

Contentment—we shouldn't leave home without it.

*Lord Jesus, give us the strength to do everything*
*we need to do each day and there discover the*
*true contentment Your Word promises. Amen.*

*"Blessed are you who hunger now,
for you will be satisfied."*

LUKE 6:21

What should we be hungry for?

The day Bob married Cheryl he weighed less than 150 pounds. The smiling young man of twenty-four in his trim brown tuxedo underwent some changes by his first anniversary—he had added almost thirty pounds to his weight. He claims it was his wife's delicious cooking that created an appetite he hadn't had as a single man.

Jesus said there is one thing we should develop a hunger for early in our lives. Listen to Eugene Peterson's beautiful paraphrase, "You're blessed when you've worked up a good appetite for God. He's food and drink in the best meal you'll ever eat" (Matthew 5:6 MSG). Why not feast daily on the rich fare of God's Word? Try reading two chapters of the Old Testament, one chapter of the New Testament, and one chapter each from the Psalms and Proverbs. This regimen takes us through the entire Bible in one year. We will have fed our souls with the bread of heaven—a several course banquet we can enjoy each day and not gain unneeded weight.

*Lord Jesus, thank You that Your Word satisfies
as nothing else can. Amen.*

*As a father has compassion on his children,*
*so the LORD has compassion on those who fear him.*

PSALM 103:13

What is a romantic care package?

When our older children were away at college, we would send them special packages during final exams. The gift boxes would include chicken soup mix, packets of instant coffee, and microwaveable popcorn. The purpose was to assure them we were thinking about them as they feverishly wrote term papers and crammed for final exams.

It isn't just our kids who need our special care and empathy; so does our spouse. Rather than filling a cardboard box with late-night snacks and powdered beverages, why not send each other notes and letters filled with expressions such as, "I am praying for you today," or "Whatever burdens your heart, burdens mine...allow me to carry it for a while." Such simple heartfelt notes won't necessarily erase their problem or resolve their painful circumstances, but it will lift their spirits and comfort their heart.

Perhaps we all need to be more careful—that is, "full of care"—for the one we love.

*Dear God, may we show each other the same*
*love and compassion You have shown us from*
*Your heart as our Father. Amen.*

*For since the creation of the world God's invisible qualities—his eternal power and divine nature—have been clearly seen.*

Romans 1:20

Can we see God in the world He created?

One research study found that a significant percentage of all men identifying themselves as a Conservative Protestant had viewed pornography in one form or another in the last month (the statistics for other religious groups had similar tragic rates). The result of this growing involvement in pornography is the loss of our ability to see God in our world.

*The Message* paraphrased the words of Jesus this way, "You're blessed when you get your inside world—your mind and heart—put right. Then you can see God in the outside world" (Matthew 5:8). When we compromise our inner purity, we lose the ability to see God in the outside world. When we repent of that sin, we are able to once again clearly gaze upon God's eternal power and divine nature.

If pornography is a problem, make the decision today to abandon it for good that God's invisible qualities might reappear on the screen of your soul.

*Dear Jesus, when confronted with impure images, may we immediately turn our eyes upon You and look full into Your wonderful face. Amen.*

*Peacemakers who sow in peace reap
a harvest of righteousness.*

JAMES 3:18

Are we an agent of peace in our home?

The typical Hebrew greeting is "Shalom!" The word literally means "Peace to you!" The term connotes far more than just the absence of conflict, but wishes that all the elements of harmony, health, and goodness be yours.

It's sad to watch a married couple spend their life together experiencing a lack of "shalom" in their relationship. Ongoing conflict vacuums the joy out of home, leaves the kids confused and insecure, and fills the relationship with regret, anger, and frustration. Jesus encouraged us all to be peacemakers, and that would include husbands and wives. Listen to one paraphrase of His words: "You're blessed when you can show people how to cooperate instead of compete or fight. That's when you discover who you really are, and your place in God's family" (Matthew 5:9 MSG).

Jesus calls every spouse to become an agent of peacemaking. We can learn to cooperate rather than compete, to collaborate instead of collide, and to agree with a listening heart rather than attack. When we learn to sow in peace, we shall surely reap a harvest of righteousness.

*Lord, make us instruments of Your peace.
Amen.*

*"Do not suppose that I have come to bring peace to the earth. I did not come to bring peace, but a sword."*

MATTHEW 10:34

Is there a price to pay for defending biblical values?

When one of our children was in elementary school, we learned his class was doing a study unit that involved the occult. As parents and believers in Jesus Christ we had a choice to make: either we could avoid causing a stir or we could object. We chose to object. Ultimately we chose to have our son sit outside his classroom and read other books. Later we chose to home-school some of our children and sent others to a private Christian school.

Jesus warned us that defending biblical values would cost us. As *The Message* puts it, "You're blessed when your commitment to God provokes persecution. The persecution drives you even deeper into God's kingdom" (Matthew 5:10). To follow Jesus in our biblical view of marriage and the values appropriate for children may cost us. The culture may misunderstand us or label our position as "hateful."

It is never hateful to speak God's Word nor prejudicial to tell the truth. It is consistent with Jesus's words, "Do not suppose that I have come to bring peace to the earth."

*Dear Jesus, may we each day be willing to pick up our cross and follow You wherever that may lead us. Amen.*

*Let your conversation be always full of
grace, seasoned with salt, so that you may
know how to answer everyone.*

COLOSSIANS 4:6

Should our conversation be salt-free?

There's no question that consuming too much sodium chloride in our diet can have harmful effects. Among other things it raises the probability of developing hypertension and other health risk factors. Yet, the Bible teaches that adding the right types of "spiritual salt" in our conversation produce numerous positive results.

So much so that the Scripture encourages us to pour on the salt. Certainly not the kind that gives us high blood pressure but instead fills our speech with grace and wisdom. The Bible refers to this as words "seasoned with salt." Instead of harsh, judgmental, or manipulative speech, we are to communicate kindness, acceptance, and honesty. As others have pointed out, salt creates thirst, preserves from decay, and brings out the savor in food.

It is crucial that in marriage our conversation create a thirst for deeper intimacy, keep our relationship from disintegrating, and bring out the savory taste of grace and love in generous portions.

*Dear Lord, let our gracious speech create a
thirst for more. Amen.*

*"I am the living bread that came down from heaven. Whoever eats this bread will live forever."*

JOHN 6:51

What can we learn from a piece of bad pizza? One evening our family ordered an extra-large pizza for supper. As we uttered the "Amen" around the table, we all reached for a huge, deep-dish slice. Suddenly Bob's mouth felt as if he had bitten into a thousand sharp pins. The red pizza sauce was rancid and therefore toxic; we had to return the entire pie for a refund.

Jesus tells us He is the exact opposite of toxic food. He is the living bread from heaven—the true delicious crust of life—and we are to feed on Him. Have we invited this Jesus into our marriage? Do we worship Him daily as a family? Is His Presence everywhere in our home?

Even the best deep-dish pizza will leave us hungry and wanting more. Jesus, the true bread of life, will satisfy the deepest hunger pangs of our soul both now and forever. No matter how we slice it, Jesus is the real deal.

*Lord Jesus, give us the true bread that has come down from above that we may never hunger in our hearts again. Amen.*

*The prudent see danger and take refuge,
but the simple keep going and pay the penalty.*

PROVERBS 27:12

Is the washing machine making noises in the basement?
Perhaps we're the only couple in the world that has
regular trouble with appliances. Trying to save money, we
purchased a used washing machine from a second-hand
appliance store. All was well until we heard from the basement something sounding like the entire percussion sec-
tion of the Ohio State University marching band. We
went downstairs to discover our new used washer was...
well, washed up.

Some rumbling problems in marriage can't be ignored
either. If a spouse is abusing alcohol or drugs, surfing the
Internet for pornography, overspending, or showing interest in another person, we must pay full attention and deal
with it. The Bible tells us the prudent see danger and do
something about it, but the foolish ignore it and pay a big
price. If we see peril ahead, we should seek help from a
Christian pastor or Bible-believing counselor. Otherwise,
the day may come when our marriage is hung out to dry.

*Heavenly Father, give us the faith to face our
dangers head-on, knowing Your courage, grace,
and wisdom will be ours. Amen.*

*"'I will set out and go back to my father and say to him:
Father, I have sinned against heaven and against you.'"*

Luke 15:18

I s it ever too early or too late to apologize?
Perhaps our anger problems have destroyed our home. Or, we may be living with ongoing regret as to how we fought with one another while raising our children. We may be tempted to believe it's too late to fix the situation and all hope is gone.

The Bible takes a different view. God's Word says it's never too late to try and seek out someone to sincerely apologize. The Prodigal Son resolved to return home and offer the needed apologies to try and restore his relationships. While we can't undo past events, a sincere apology can open the way to a new future for us and those we love.

It all begins by learning to quickly admit our wrongs and freely say the words, "I am sorry. I was wrong. Please forgive me."

*Lord Jesus, help us swallow our pride and
apologize when we have offended others.
Amen.*

*Jesus Christ is the same yesterday and today and forever.*

HEBREWS 13:8

What's the glue that sticks for fifty years?

We attended a marriage conference where a prize was offered for the couple married the longest. The free dinner was won by a couple that had stayed together forty-one years. When the husband was asked the secret of their nearly five-decade bond, he simply replied, "Christ."

Too often we can try to glue together a lasting marriage with the inferior epoxy of common goals, physical attraction, or financial investments. However, when adversity strikes we discover how easily it can tear apart the fabric of our relationship. There is no bonding agent as powerful and reliable as Jesus Christ Himself. The book of Hebrews promises He is the same yesterday, today, and forever. It is precisely His unchanging character and unfailing love that can hold the two of us together through illnesses, layoffs, downsizing, upheaval, and even tragedies.

When we make Jesus the glue of our marriage, we discover nothing on earth can tear the two of us apart. Jesus is the ultimate adhesive for adversity.

*Lord Jesus, thank You that no pressure of*
*hardship is so strong that You are not*
*stronger still. Amen.*

*Now as the church submits to Christ, so also wives should submit to their husbands in everything.*

EPHESIANS 5:24

Is submission exploitation?

Perhaps the most misunderstood word in the Bible is *submission*. To some it is synonymous with oppression, bondage, or exploitation. That's unfortunate because submission actually means, "to voluntarily yield in love." A wife is called to submit to her husband for the high and holy purpose of allowing his Christlike leadership traits to emerge. Just as Jesus cannot provide and care for the church if it does not submit to Him, a husband cannot bless the life of a wife unless she is willing to honor and respect his leadership. Her willing submission frees her husband to fulfill all the sacrificial duties Christ has called him to in the marriage.

Scripture promises a great blessing when we submit to Christ. The promised favor of God is upon a wife who voluntarily yields in love to her husband. She opens the way for the Lord to bless her life in countless ways. Submission is not subjugation, but God's path to true freedom and fulfillment in marriage.

*Lord Jesus, grant us the trust, faith,
and willingness to submit to You
in everything we do. Amen.*

*Through Jesus, therefore, let us continually
offer to God a sacrifice of praise—the fruit
of lips that openly profess his name.*

HEBREWS 13:15

Is there help for depression?

Depression can rob us of our joy, energy, and sense of purpose in life. Certainly depression can cause a marriage to suffer. Tim LaHaye, well-known author and speaker, believes anger and self-pity are two primary causes of depression. We first get angry and then feel sorry for ourselves, and together they produce sadness and despair. The cure for depression is to choose the polar opposites of anger and self-pity—forgiveness and gratitude. We can't stay angry when we forgive someone, and we can't feel sorry for ourselves if we are rejoicing in God.

Scripture tells us to continually offer to God a sacrifice of praise. Such rejoicing clears the mind of dark and brooding thoughts and cleanses the soul of hopeless and life-numbing emotions.

Why not try a seven-day test of exercising forgiveness and thankfulness? See if they don't spark an inner rally that will help us come out of even a great depression.

*Lord Jesus, how we thank You that "no pit is so
deep that Your love is not deeper still." Amen.*

*"If your right eye causes you to stumble, gouge
it out and throw it away. It is better for you
to lose one part of your body than for your
whole body to be thrown into hell."*

MATTHEW 5:29

What is a radical response to defeat radical temptation?

A husband finds himself giving a second glance
toward a female coworker. A wife occasionally flirts with
the husband of her best friend. Regardless of the specif-
ics of the situation, once we start down the road of temptation, if we stay the course only ruin lies ahead. Because
direction is destiny, unless we make a sharp course correction now, we will one day find ourselves caught in adultery
(it's not a matter of *if* but *when* this will happen).

That's why Jesus made the shocking statement if our
right eye causes us to sin, we should gouge it out. He
wasn't talking about self-harm but taking radical steps
to deal with radical temptation. Applied to marriage, we
immediately break off all contact, fantasizing, and conversations with the other person and enter into an accountability relationship with a mature believer. Once we
change direction we change our destiny—with no regrets.

*Heavenly Father, there is no price too great
for us to preserve our character and the honor
of Your Name. Amen.*

*Flee from sexual immorality. All other sins a
person commits are outside the body, but whoever
sins sexually, sins against their own body.*

1 Corinthians 6:18

When is the right time to break off an affair?

One man told us his wife had admitted to having an affair, but she asked for a little more time to break it off. "Be patient," she said, "it's almost over." We've seldom heard of such a ridiculous request. Anyone who is serious about ending an illicit relationship will do it right now.

The devil always provides one more reason to stay one more day in a sinful relationship. Scripture tells us to "flee from sexual immorality," and that means right now—not tomorrow. Adultery is sin, and God judges sin, yet He also offers His immediate grace and mercy to those who turn from it. If we've fallen into sin in a relationship, we must not delay. We need to put on our best running shoes and sprint as fast as we can in the other direction. God will provide the wind at your back.

*Lord Jesus, keep us from the foolish belief that
we can stay and outsmart sin. Give us the
grace to quickly flee. Amen.*

*"Don't call me Naomi," she told them. "Call me Mara,*
*because the Almighty has made my life very bitter."*

Ruth 1:20

Does God seem silent these days?

Bruce Wilkinson tells the story of a Christian woman who told him that God had seemed distant most of her life. He asked her if she was bitter toward anyone. At first she couldn't think of anyone, but then admitted she had some hard feelings toward her mother. He urged her to go home and make a list of her resentments. The next day she returned with twelve pages of notes. He led her through a prayer of repentance and forgiveness toward her mother. The next day she returned with a glowing smile to say she now sensed the presence of God for the first time in years.

In the book of Ruth, an elderly woman named Naomi was embittered toward God. She even suggested her named be changed to Mara, which means "bitter." Are we bitter toward someone today? We must confess that to God as sin and turn from it. Bitterness could be robbing us of life's most precious experience—the nearness of God.

*Lord Jesus, take from our hearts this very hour*
*every vestige of settled anger, resentment, and*
*unforgiveness. Amen.*

*Accept one another, then, just as Christ accepted
you, in order to bring praise to God.*

Romans 15:7

What keeps us from accepting our spouse?

We talked with a man who expressed resentment that his wife was overweight. "I'd like to say I love her," he lamented, "but I just can't say it. Not with the way she looks right now." The truth is if he doesn't love his spouse just as she is today, he won't love her more when she weighs ninety-eight pounds. Love is not based on appearance but what is in our hearts. It is our unconditional acceptance of the other person even if they have issues with health, appearance, or sexual performance.

Paul tells us to accept each other in the same way Christ has accepted us. Did Christ say He would accept us when we straightened up our life, went to church more often, or lost weight? No, He lavished His accepting grace on us even if when we were sinners—perhaps at the worst point in our lives.

Real love transcends the externals and accepts one another just as we are.

*Lord and Savior, thank You for loving me just
as I am—without one plea. Amen.*

*"I, even I, am he who blots out
your transgressions, for my own sake,
and remembers your sins no more."*

ISAIAH 43:25

How can we forgive when we can't forget?

So often we hear, "I would like to forgive, but I just can't forget." The good news is that true forgiveness doesn't require forgetting, but as Neil Anderson points out, we must release the other person from the moral debt they owe us. We must give up seeking revenge or retribution and instead give the hurt and pain that person caused to Jesus to bear for us.

Whenever we inwardly struggle with the memory of someone's past failure toward us, it's usually a caution sign we haven't forgiven them. Once we do truly release them from all moral debts and all desire to pay them back, a real change soon occurs in our hearts. We may still remember the incident, but it has lost its barbed hook and doesn't wound our soul anymore. It becomes just another fact of record, no longer holding power over our mind or emotions.

Forget forgetting and choose real forgiveness instead.

*Dear Jesus, thank You for Your divine
forgiveness that refuses to use our
past sins against us. Amen.*

*"What do you people mean by quoting this*
*proverb about the land of Israel:*
*'The fathers eat sour grapes,*
*and the children's teeth are set on edge'?"*

EZEKIEL 18:2

Why are kids as happy as their parents' marriage? We've noticed a powerful pattern through the years. When married couples get along well and enjoy each other's company, their kids tend to turn out to be positive and optimistic people. When spouses continually fight, bicker, and belittle each other, their kids tend to turn out angry and critical people.

It reminds us of an often quoted proverb in ancient Israel, "The fathers eat sour grapes, and the children's teeth are set on edge." The impact of our parental attitudes and behavior on our children is enormous. Each day we are chiseling into their young souls either good or bad messages—primarily from the quality of our marriage.

If we've set a negative example for our children, it's never too late to alter course. Our change of heart toward one another will transform their attitude for a lifetime and may even put an end to sour grapes.

*Dear Jesus, help us to remember we are the*
*first Bible our children will ever read. Amen.*

*Humble yourselves, therefore, under God's mighty*
*hand, that he may lift you up in due time.*

1 Peter 5:6

How can humility save a marriage?

From time to time we hear angry and disillusioned spouses say, "It's too late. My marriage is so over. Nothing can save it now." We often respond, "No, your marriage is not over yet. There is still a way to rescue it. But it will be difficult."

"But how?" they ask.

"It will require you to humble yourself."

Humility is our willingness to put God and the other person above ourselves in loving service. While difficult to do, it has an extraordinary power all its own to change hearts. People may argue with our logic, mock our passion, or laugh at our words, but they will find it extremely difficult to resist our humility. If we put God and our spouse above ourselves and serve them as Jesus served others, their hardened heart may begin to melt.

If we have come to the place where we want to throw in the towel, why not use it instead to wash our spouse's feet?

*Dear Jesus, whenever we need to understand*
*the true nature of humility, turn our eyes to*
*the cross. Amen.*

*"I am the vine; you are the branches. If you remain in me and I in you, you will bear much fruit; apart from me you can do nothing."*

JOHN 15:5

Are we bearing fruit or simply growing flowers? We once moved into a home that was beautifully landscaped with a variety of bushes, shrubs, and trees. While the beauty of our backyard was amazing to behold, it produced only flowers—never any fruit.

How many of our lives are like that? We spend our time, money, and energy on temporary things such as vacations, furniture, or the latest fashions. While the end result may be impressive to behold, it contains little or no spiritual yield. Jesus said, "Apart from me you can do nothing (of eternal value)." On the other hand, if we abide in Christ by serving others, sharing our faith, and loving the unlovely, Jesus promised we will bear much fruit— fruit that will remain for all eternity.

So what will it be in our life as a couple—flowers or fruit? The choice is ours.

*Lord Jesus, thank You that all branches have to do is remain connected to the Vine to bear fruit. Keep us abiding in You. Amen.*

*Therefore, as God's chosen people, holy and
dearly loved, clothe yourselves with compassion,
kindness, humility, gentleness and patience.*

COLOSSIANS 3:12

Are we dressed for spiritual success?

Business magazines will tell you that to succeed in life you have to dress the part. In a successful marriage, a winning spiritual wardrobe means clothing ourselves with compassion, kindness, humility, gentleness, and patience. We are God's chosen people that are holy and dearly loved by our heavenly Father. Secure in this knowledge, we can treat our spouse with the virtues we are clothed with by God.

Dressing for spiritual success may also require us to discard some items from our wardrobe. Worn out and useless clothes include detachment, impatience, pride, harshness, and a quick temper. Putting on the right wardrobe daily results in a growing marriage where our spouse more deeply loves and respects us, believes our faith is genuine, and desires to model our spiritual behavior. They will be drawn to the inner person God is making us.

The good news is that if we dress for spiritual success, it never goes out of fashion.

*Heavenly Father, may we put on Christ each
morning that the world might behold Him in
all His love and glory. Amen.*

*But the fruit of the Spirit is love, joy, peace, forbearance, kindness, goodness, faithfulness, gentleness and self-control. Against such things there is no law.*

GALATIANS 5:22-23

Did we lose our patience recently?

Let's take this simple test: think back on all the times we lost our patience with our spouse or family members. How many of those sad incidents do we now regret? Now let's recall all the times we showed calm and forbearance toward our partner or kids. How many of those patient responses do we regret today? It's a good guess that we have remorse over the times we lost our patience and gratitude for those moments we displayed a calm and serene attitude.

The truth is we lose more than we know when we lose our patience: we forfeit peace with ourselves, with our spouse, and worst of all with our God. Unbridled anger usually leaves everyone feeling worse for the incident, and it will often take time to repair the relationship. But the fruit of the Holy Spirit produces attitudes, words, and behaviors marked by patience and forbearance—virtues that leave no regrets.

*Heavenly Father, we thank You for Your loving patience that led us to salvation. Amen.*

*God presented Christ as a sacrifice of atonement,
through the shedding of his blood—to be
received by faith. He did this to demonstrate his
righteousness, because in his forbearance he had
left the sins committed beforehand unpunished.*

ROMANS 3:25

What virtue closely resembles the grace of God?

In Bob's college dorm a lot of teasing and practical jokes went on—typically in a spirit of innocent fun and friendship. When confronted with a put-down, he learned to counter with, "Hey, I resemble that remark." The retort proved so effective that it usually ended the teasing.

Forbearance is the demonstration of patient tolerance in the face of an offense. It closely resembles the grace of God simply because it returns something good for something bad. God in His forbearance left our former sins unpunished, and instead put forward Christ as the atonement for sin. When we display forbearance, it is evidence that we are under the control of the Holy Spirit.

Next time someone hits us with a verbal zinger simply smile and say, "Hey, I resemble that remark," and watch them search for words.

*Lord Jesus, we thank You for Your forbearance
that offered us life when we deserved death for
our sins. Amen.*

*A person's wisdom yields patience;*
*it is to one's glory to overlook an offense.*

PROVERBS 19:11

What should we be willing to overlook?

There are times to challenge the bad behavior of others and times to overlook their conduct. How to know the difference? Our rule of thumb is this: If someone's conduct violates our healthy boundaries, it needs to be challenged. If it is simply a careless remark or a thoughtless deed (and by no means a pattern), it is to our honor to overlook it.

Notice the Bible says it is wisdom, not weakness or passivity that gives us the ability to overlook foolish and petty offenses. Wisdom is applying God's eternal truth in an appropriate manner to our situation. Whenever we overlook an offense, it is to our glory—and more importantly, the glory of God. It demonstrates Christ's controlling presence in our lives. It demonstrates an inner insight nurtured by God's Word.

Overlooking small offenses usually results in a number of positive outcomes: communication is eventually restored, tumultuous emotions are settled down, and true reconciliation occurs.

*Dear Jesus, You have overlooked so much in*
*our lives and all to Your glory. Teach us to do*
*the same with one another. Amen.*

*Whoever conceals their sins does not prosper,*
*but the one who confesses and*
*renounces them finds mercy.*

PROVERBS 28:13

If our child made the worst mistake of their lives, could they dare tell us?

We made a deal with our teenagers. If they were ever to find themselves in a place they should not be, or doing something they should not be doing, they could call us anytime day or night. We would immediately come and pick them up with no questions asked (at least for the moment). We never wanted them to refrain from seeking our help for fear of our overreaction.

We all pray that our children will make the right choices in life. But what if they should make a bad choice or even a horrible decision? Will we be the first person they turn to for help? Yes, if they have witnessed us demonstrate patience with one another and offer mercy in the aftermath of our failures. Our example of grace will, we hope, give them the confidence they need to share their bad choices with us.

*Lord Jesus, may our children never feel they*
*must conceal their sins from us, but rather*
*know if they confess them, they will find mercy.*
*Amen.*

*Above all, love each other deeply, because*
*love covers over a multitude of sins.*

1 PETER 4:8

What does it mean to cover our sins?

"I'll admit it," one young husband said to us, "my heart has hardened toward my wife. So what should I do?" He saw no resolution except to start over with someone new.

Fortunately, God has a much better alternative: to let love cover over a multitude of sins. It doesn't mean one spouse deliberately ignores the wrongdoing of the other, or tries to revise what happened and give it a positive spin. Rather, it means we spread love over the sins of another person the way we would spread a goose-down quilt over our spouse in the winter to keep them warm. Something good is laid over something bad—it is an act of grace.

When our spouse covers us with love, we are drawn toward them. It often will create conviction, and we see our need to forsake our sinful attitude or behavior. Ultimately God is free to bring about true reconciliation and intimacy.

Is it time to blanket one another with love?

*Dear Jesus, let us love one another deeply from*
*our hearts. Amen.*

*May our Lord Jesus Christ himself and God our
Father, who loved us and by his grace gave us eternal
encouragement and good hope, encourage your hearts
and strengthen you in every good deed and word.*

2 Thessalonians 2:16

Can we give our spouse too much encouragement?
We all meet people at work, in the store, and
even next door who are struggling with hidden difficulties,
sometimes even tragedies. Encouragement is that wonderful gift that strengthens the heart of someone struggling
with the problems of life. It literally brings courage back
into the heart of someone who is drawn down with confusion, anxiety, or despair.

Wives can struggle with all the competing expectations that come with marriage and raising children. Husbands can labor with the burden of providing for their
families and balancing time between work and home. We
all need encouragement from our partner. The good news
is that God is the source of all true encouragement. He
pours it into our lives so we can share the overflow with
others.

Don't worry about overdoing encouragement—it
simply cannot be overdone.

*Dear Jesus, help us find a word of courage to
lift up the hands and strengthen the knees of
someone who is faltering. Amen.*

*For everything that was written in the past*
*was written to teach us, so that through the*
*endurance taught in the Scriptures and the*
*encouragement they provide we might have hope.*

ROMANS 15:4

What always hits the target in marriage?

The story is told of a tourist traveling in the country who noticed a barn painted with five large targets—each with an arrow sticking dead center in the bull's-eye. Curious, he turned into the driveway and found a young boy stringing his bow. "That's some impressive shooting, young man," the tourist said. "How do you do it?"

"It's simple," the boy said with a grin. "Every time I shoot an arrow and hit the barn, I just climb up and paint a target around it."

That's not a bad metaphor for offering encouragement in marriage. Each time our spouse takes aim to improve themselves, we should run up and paint a target around wherever their arrow lands. The Bible says things written in the past were meant to encourage us today. Let's use God's encouraging Word to give new heart to our spouse today. Encouragement hits the bull's-eye every time.

*Lord Jesus, thank You that Your holy Word*
*was written in pen and ink as a permanent*
*source of hope and encouragement. Amen.*

*Who provides food for the raven*
*when its young cry out to God*
*and wander about for lack of food?*

JOB 38:41

W ho is our Provider?
It was a rainy day in September, and we were in need of groceries for supper. The car was unavailable, and it was too wet to ride a bike to the local store. Going into the garage to clean up, we spotted a cooler from a recent fishing trip. We opened the lid and found an abundance of unused canned goods and boxes of prepackaged food— just what we needed to provide for a full and delicious supper that night. It was one more example of God's provision, albeit from an unexpected source.

One of the names for God in the Old Testament is *Jehovah Jireh*—"The Lord Who Provides." Scriptures tell us God even provides food for the raven's young when they cry out to Him. Certainly we are of much greater value than the birds, so we can be confident in God's daily care for our lives.

Has the Lord met our needs today? Then we should tell someone the details of His great faithfulness toward us.

*Dear God, morning, noon, and evening we*
*thank You for Your provision. Amen.*

*For I do not want to see you now and make*
*only a passing visit; I hope to spend some*
*time with you, if the Lord permits.*

1 Corinthians 16:7

D o we seek God for His needed permits?

A house for sale was badly in need of repair and stood vacant for several months. It was finally purchased by someone intending to rehab it and flip it. The day finally arrived when the work started, and then suddenly all construction on the site ceased. No one returned to the house for weeks. Only later did the neighbors learn the owner had not acquired the necessary building permits from the village.

To operate properly, a builder needs the right permits. In much the same way—whatever events or plans we might have, we should qualify them with these crucial four words: "If the Lord permits." We must recognize that God in His sovereignty chooses what will happen and what will not. His lordship determines what we encounter and what we will not. Jesus taught us to pray, "Not my will, but yours be done." That's another way of saying in our prayers, "If the Lord permits."

*Heavenly Father, we want to live and make*
*plans for each day fully aware they will occur*
*only if You should allow. Amen.*

*The LORD God said, "It is not good for the man to*
*be alone. I will make a helper suitable for him…"*
*Then the LORD God made a woman from the rib he had*
*taken out of the man, and he brought her to the man.*

GENESIS 2:18,22

Who introduced the first couple?
Up to 40 percent of all singles use online dating sites to meet prospective life mates. While such Internet match-making companies can pair people of similar interests and values, for the believer, who actually leads us to our future spouse? According to the Genesis account, the Lord made a woman from one of the man's ribs, and "he brought her to the man." Did you notice that? God Himself introduced the first couple.

It is our conviction that God is in the same business today. If we make knowing and serving Christ our first priority in life, we can trust God to bring the right person into our life. Which of the matchmaking sites do we recommend? BibleGateway.com (or a similar site) that will lead you into God's Word each and every day.

*Dear Jesus, thank You for introducing us to*
*each other. Amen.*

*For physical training is of some value, but*
*godliness has value for all things, holding promise*
*for both the present life and the life to come.*

1 Timothy 4:8

How do we stay in good spiritual shape?

There's the story of a man who ate too much junk food. When he went to his doctor for his annual physical, the man asked, "So how do I stand?"

"That's what I'd like to know," said the doctor in dismay.

The Bible tells us physical training is of some value, but godliness holds promise both for this life and the world to come. What is godliness? As one Bible dictionary defines it, "Godliness is the reverent awareness of God's sovereignty over every aspect of life, and the attendant determination to honor Him in all one's conduct." That means God rules our lives, and we are to honor Him in everything we say and do.

Yet godliness is one of those traits that also require practice and daily discipline. To get in proper spiritual shape demands daily surrender to the Lordship of Christ and measuring all our behavior against the example of Jesus.

*Dear Jesus, begin a spiritual fitness program*
*to prepare us both for today and for eternity.*
*Amen.*

*Let beer be for those who are perishing,*
*wine for those who are in anguish!*
*Let them drink and forget their poverty*
*and remember their misery no more.*

PROVERBS 31:6-7

What is self-medication?

We know of people living with deep emotional and spiritual pain. They attempt to alleviate their inner anguish through self-medication, using self-destructive behaviors to make the pain go away temporarily. This may include drug and alcohol abuse, overeating and overspending, pornography, and even an affair.

Proverbs facetiously says alcohol should be given to those who are in anguish so they will forget their problems. But while it can distract from our pain, it will not resolve it. The answer lies in letting the love of God heal our inner wounds.

How can God do that? We must confess before God that we are helpless to stop self-medicating all on our own. Next, we forgive others (and ourselves) for the hurts we have created. Finally, we turn to Jesus in prayer to find our true value and the love that can heal our hearts. It's time to cancel our prescription for self-medication and let the Great Physician do the healing.

*Lord Jesus, thank You that You have come to*
*bind up the brokenhearted and set the captive*
*free. Amen.*

*At the end of your life you will groan,*
*when your flesh and body are spent.*
*You will say, "How I hated discipline!*
*How my heart spurned correction!"*

PROVERBS 5:11-12

How is imagination a key to defeating temptation? Victory over temptation doesn't just happen—it is always the result of our intentional attitudes and actions. We can use imagination as a powerful tool in gaining victory over temptation when it strikes.

First, imagine having to confess our sexual sin to our spouse, children, and close friends. Second, imagine the personal shame, regret, and humiliation that will occur once our actions are known. Third, imagine the complications of a sexual disease or a pregnancy out of wedlock. Fourth, imagine the pain of losing our marriage and many of the close relationships we now enjoy. And fifth, imagine the final day when we will look Jesus Christ in the eye to explain our actions.

Imagining one or more of these painful consequences will take the allure out of temptation.

*Lord Jesus, help us to imagine the consequences*
*of sin in order to destroy its appeal and allure.*
*Amen.*

*Then I acknowledged my sin to you and did not cover
up my iniquity. I said, "I will confess my transgressions
to the LORD." And you forgave the guilt of my sin.*

PSALM 32:5

What if our marriage began in sin?

Some couples have told us they began their marriage in disobedience to God. "We were living together before marriage," they say. Or, "There was no biblical justification for our prior divorce and remarriage. Does that mean God will not bless our marriage or that we should divorce?"

No, the Bible does not counsel ending a marriage because of its wrong beginnings. Two wrongs do not make a right. Instead, sincerely confess the prior sin to God and receive His full forgiveness. Then apologize to those most wounded by the sinful actions. Finally, dedicate the marriage to the service and glory of God.

If we cover up our iniquity, it will lead to struggle and suffering in our lives. But if we confess our wrong start to God, He will forgive the guilt of our sin.

*Lord Jesus, thank You that "there is a fountain
filled with blood drawn from Immanuel's veins,
and sinners plunged beneath that flood lose all
their guilty stains." Amen.*

*Jesus looked at them and said, "With man this is impossible, but not with God; all things are possible with God."*

MARK 10:27

W hy do couples stay stuck for a lifetime?
Sadly many couples spend a great deal of their married life feeling distant and unfulfilled in the relationship. They've tried a number of things that haven't worked. Why can't they make any progress?

There are a variety of possible reasons, including: one partner's commitment to the marriage may not be the same as their spouse's; change takes hard work and one or both may be too lazy to make the effort; they have believed lies about themselves or the other person; or they fail to turn to God and instead rely on their own strength to improve things.

Thankfully, real change is still possible even after years of being stuck. Start by humbling yourselves before God and asking for His help. Then substitute the truth of God's Word for the falsehoods you have believed. Finally, realize the pain of staying the same is greater than the pain of changing.

Take heart—with God all things are possible.

*Lord Jesus, we are ready to move onward and upward. Lead us on, O King Eternal. Amen.*

*Didn't the LORD make you one with your wife?*
*In body and spirit you are his. And what does he*
*want? Godly children from your union. So guard*
*your heart; remain loyal to the wife of your youth.*

MALACHI 2:15 NLT

What are the free gifts we can give our children? Parents often believe that what their children want most are expensive toys, adoring attention, or a truckload of money. But what they really want from us can't be purchased, printed, or pretended.

The first free gift is to pass on our faith in Jesus Christ (though our children must eventually accept Christ for themselves). The second gift is for us as spouses to love each other. A mountain of research proves that children from intact, loving, two-parent families outperform in almost every area of life.

So why not offer our children what they need most to succeed in life? Let's start now by sharing our faith in Jesus regularly with our kids. Then let's affirm our love for our spouse before our children openly and affectionately. Our kids may not turn out to be perfect, but they will likely turn out steady, secure, and thankful.

*Dear God, make us one so it will be easier for*
*our children to believe in Your loving Father*
*heart. Amen.*

*"Then you will know the truth, and*
*the truth will set you free."*

JOHN 8:32

What deceptions do we believe?

One of the chief obstacles to a fulfilling marriage is wrong thinking. If we believe false ideas about ourselves or our spouse, trouble follows—particularly when we act on those falsehoods. The Bible tells us the devil is the author of all lies. If he can get us to believe his prevarications, he can control portions of our thinking and behavior.

Here are some of his common deceptions: "Your spouse is the true troubles in your life—get rid of them and you'll be free of your problems." "Nothing will ever change in your marriage, so why not give up and start over with someone new?" "You two can build a happy marriage without God, so ignore reading the Bible or praying together."

The Bible teaches us to challenge falsehoods with God's Word—that's how their power is broken. Why not make a list of the lies we contend with and compare them to the precious promises of Scripture? That will lead to lasting freedom.

*Heavenly Father, thank You that all*
*deception can be exposed and defeated*
*through Your revealed Word. Amen.*

*And now these three remain: faith, hope and*
*love. But the greatest of these is love.*

1 CORINTHIANS 13:13

Is it time to quit focusing on problems?

One secular marriage writer believes spending time on solving our marriage problems is a big mistake. While working on our difficulties may bring some improvement, it still won't create a fulfilling marriage. Rather, he believes we should focus on creating love—building a deep soul connection between the two of us.

Some two thousand years ago, the apostle Paul shared that same conclusion with believers in Corinth, many of whom were struggling with marriage issues. He makes the bold assertion that love is the greatest of all (1 Corinthians 13:13).

How do we go about connecting with our spouse's heart with love? The author suggests (and Scripture affirms) that we need to reach out to our spouse through loving touch, loving words, and our loving presence. We should make our spouse the first priority in our life (after God). Finally, we should reenact the loving behaviors and gestures of our courtship days and do them all again.

*Heavenly Father, help us take our eyes off*
*our problems and work first and foremost on*
*restoring love to our relationship. Amen.*

*But one thing I do: Forgetting what is behind
and straining toward what is ahead, I press on
toward the goal to win the prize for which God
has called me heavenward in Christ Jesus.*

PHILIPPIANS 3:13-14

C an we leave the "what ifs" of life behind us?
We can fail to enjoy our marriage if we remain prisoners of our past doubts. We do so when we look at life
through a rearview mirror and spend countless hours asking, *Would I have been happier, wealthier, or more in love if
I had chosen someone else?* Such a retro perspective can rob
us of energy, joy, and vision to create what could be.

To break free we must first ask God's forgiveness for
trying to escape our present. Next, by faith we should
accept His promise that He can take our mess and make
it our message. Then we should cultivate an attitude of
gratitude for the person God gave us to share life's journey. Finally, we should haul life's rearview mirror out to
the trash—and not look back.

*Lord and Savior, may we never take our eyes
off the future prize to which God has called us
heavenward. Amen.*

*All kinds of animals...are being tamed and have been
tamed by mankind, but no human being can tame
the tongue. It is a restless evil, full of deadly poison.*

JAMES 3:7-8

Does the Bible address verbal abuse?

One of the most damaging behaviors in marriage is verbal abuse—the deliberate use of harsh words to inflict pain, intimidation, or humiliation on someone. Wounded mates are often at a loss how to stop their mistreatment.

Does the Bible speak to this problem? Yes it does. The book of James warns that the tongue can be as dangerous as a wild animal or bottle of poison. These are strong words and indicate just how seriously God considers the misuse (abuse) of our words.

What should we tell someone if they are being verbally abused? First, realize abuse has no place in a marriage. Next, encourage the abused spouse to never tolerate it again by responding, "Please stop. I will not accept this behavior any longer." Should the other spouse continue the abuse, walk out of the room. In serious cases it may require leaving the house and calling the police. The point is God wants it to stop.

*Dear Jesus, may the words of our mouth be
acceptable in Your sight. Amen.*

*Listen to advice and accept discipline,*
*and at the end you will be counted among the wise.*

PROVERBS 19:20

Where can we find good role models for marriage? We may have reached adulthood without ever having witnessed up close a healthy marriage. We may have grown up in a distressed, divorced, or dysfunctional home where the modeling was just the opposite.

Thankfully it's never too late for us to gain needed tools by seeking out positive resources. We can start by finding an older godly couple that will formally or informally mentor us. We can attend a marriage conference yearly to receive new skills, insights, and motivation. We can study the loving marriages found in Scripture, such as Abraham and Sarah, Aquila and Priscilla, and Joseph and Mary.

What we'll observe in good marriages is that neither person is perfect, but both partners communicate freely, give and receive forgiveness quickly, and support each other intentionally. Now is the time to learn these vital skills by seeking out godly role models and accepting wise instruction from others. There's no need for us to miss out on the blessings of a positive marriage. While we cannot change our ancestors, we can change our descendants.

*Dear Jesus, fill in what was lacking in our*
*home with Your wisdom, knowledge, and love.*
*Amen.*

*It is a trap to dedicate something rashly
and only later to consider one's vows.*

Proverbs 20:25

What about remarriage after the death of a spouse?
If we are married long enough, sadly the day will
eventually come when one of us must say good-bye to the
other. The death of one's spouse is one of life's most devastating experiences. Insurance statistics tell us that 75 percent of all widows will never remarry. On the other hand,
80 percent of widowed men will remarry—most within
two years of their loss.

Here are issues to consider before remarrying: Have
I waited long enough to complete the full grieving process? Am I prepared for my next spouse to not necessarily
accept my adult children? Am I willing to sacrifice regular
contact with my grandchildren if my next spouse wants
to live elsewhere? How can I be certain of the other person's motivation for marrying me? Will I stay committed
to the new marriage if it is less fulfilling than my first one?

Scripture cautions us we shouldn't make rash decisions only to later reconsider our vows.

*Heavenly Father, when that sad time of parting
comes, please be a lamp to our feet and
a light to our path. Amen.*

*When Sarah was 127 years old, she
died…in the land of Canaan…
Abraham married another wife, whose name
was Keturah. She gave birth to Zimran, Jokshan,
Medan, Midian, Ishbak and Shuah.*

GENESIS 23:1-2; 25:1-2 NLT

W hat are ground rules for second marriages?
The issues that need to be addressed in establishing a second marriage can be quite different from those of a first marriage. They are more complicated because both spouses bring with them a life history that includes a former marriage that may have produced children and grandchildren.

Couples who believe a second marriage creates a blank slate are often denying several realities: Children from a first marriage will need to be acknowledged, accepted, and affirmed. The blending of families will validate the old adage that blood is thicker than water. Gaining the respect of our second spouse's children will need to be more earned than granted. When there are discipline issues, the biological parent will need to take the lead.

A second marriage is less like pushing the delete button on our computer and far more like cutting and pasting our old life *into* the new.

*Lord Jesus, grant those living in a second marriage
the special grace they need to succeed and for their
children and grandchildren to prosper. Amen.*

*"There are three things that are too amazing for me,*
*four that I do not understand...*
*[one is] the way of a man with a young woman."*

PROVERBS 30:18-19

Can infatuation be real love, self-centered feelings, or a terrible lie?

The day will come when we will need to discuss with our children the incredible power of infatuation. We believe the following advice is worth sharing.

The hormones that produce our feelings of infatuation contain no intelligence, wisdom, or virtue—in other words, they cannot be trusted. If used rightly, they can help lead us to a God-glorifying relationship with a person of the opposite sex. If corrupted by our sinful human nature, they can draw us into a self-focused relationship. Worse yet, if co-opted by our enemy, they will steer us into a forbidden liaison.

To keep hormones from undoing our life when infatuation strikes, seek out the counsel of Scripture, lay the matter before God in prayer, and pursue the advice of mature believers. Remember, lasting love is built upon depth of character not the intense pull of emotions.

*Dear Jesus, help our children when infatuation*
*occurs to choose to walk in obedience to You*
*and trust their faith. Amen.*

*Also, if two lie down together, they will keep warm.*
*But how can one keep warm alone?*

ECCLESIASTES 4:11

Do we know one of our husband's best kept secrets? Perhaps the least understood fact about men is that they are lonely. When God created Adam, He said, "It is not good for the man to be alone." Most men, if they are honest, will admit they do not have one close friend. Women have trouble believing this and see men as naturally aloof. That's where they may be mistaken. It's not because men prefer to be alone that they lead solitary lives. It's because males have more difficulty forming close relationships than women do.

Wives who understand this have a great opportunity to become their husband's best friend. However, it will require they enter their husband's world more as a man would enter it—as a buddy. Consider riding along on your husband's errands, joining him in work tasks, or watching the game together. Men may not say it, but snuggling up next to him will mean the world. They cannot keep warm all alone.

*Lord Jesus, thank You for creating a place in*
*a man's heart that only a loving wife can fill.*
*Amen.*

*For this command is a lamp, this teaching is a light,*
*and correction and instruction are the way to life,*
*keeping you from your neighbor's wife,*
*from the smooth talk of a wayward woman.*

PROVERBS 6:23-24

What is the fallacy of the greener grass syndrome? Why are we tempted to believe the grass is greener on the other side of the fence? Why does the devil try to get us to buy the fantasy that there's more love, romance, or sexual thrills to be found with someone else? While a new lover can bring temporary infatuation, our same heart problems will soon resurface: selfishness, unresolved inner pain, and wrong thinking. Given time, we will soon experience the exact frustrations that led to the dissolution of our first marriage.

The antidote to the greener grass syndrome is to heed the commands of the Lord and the corrections of discipline found in Scripture. Deception is broken by truth and truth is gained by saturating our heart and mind daily with God's Word.

*Lord Jesus, may the truth of Your Word build*
*hedges around our marriage so high, deep,*
*and wide that no power of hell can break*
*through. Amen.*

*If it is possible, as far as it depends on
you, live at peace with everyone.*

ROMANS 12:18

How can we be at peace with someone unwilling to reconcile?

When our relationship is disrupted by someone else's sin or offense against us, we have an obligation to forgive. However, the command to "live at peace with everyone" implies that it takes two individuals to reconcile. What if we are willing but the other person is not? Does God hold us accountable for the unreconciled relationship?

If the other person flatly refuses to admit their wrong or to express remorse, there is little more for us to do than pray for them. Then we are free from our responsibility in the matter and can leave the matter in God's hands. While we must maintain openness toward future reconciliation we can live with the peace of mind that we have done all we can for now. Maintaining proper boundaries is vital so that the other person cannot continue to offend or harm us. God will set all things right when Christ returns, and we may just have to patiently wait for that day for final reconciliation to occur.

*Heavenly Father, grant us the wisdom to know
the things we can change in a relationship and
those we cannot change. Amen.*

*But among you there must not be even a hint of sexual
immorality, or of any kind of impurity, or of greed,
because these are improper for God's holy people.*

EPHESIANS 5:3

Is there a connection between premarital sex and adultery?

Whenever adultery occurs, complete with its soul-searing confusion, needless betrayal, and painful heartbreak, comes the question, "How did I end up with a cheating spouse?"

One explanation we believe that has been largely ignored is the presence of premarital sexual activity. A person willing to engage in premarital sex can become a high risk to engage in sex outside of marriage. The reason is character—the same lack of character that led to premarital sex is the same deficit of virtue that produces extramarital sex. That's why if there is premarital sexual experiences in a couple's history, it needs to be confessed as sin today—not just the act itself, but the lack of character that produced it.

Scripture offers a remedy for our character impurity, and it is called holiness. If we will consecrate our life, marriage, and character to the sanctifying work of the Holy Spirit, we will be planting the best hedge against adultery available.

*Dear Jesus, make us holy as You are holy.
Amen.*

*And Jacob noticed that [his father-in-law] Laban's attitude toward him was not what it had been.*

GENESIS 31:2

What's the answer to rejection by in-laws?

One of marriage's thorniest issues is trouble with the in-laws. In the book of Genesis, we learn Jacob struggled with his father-in-law, Laban. Laban's sons falsely accused Jacob of stealing their father's wealth. The Bible says then that Laban's "attitude toward [Jacob] was not what it had been."

Thankfully, Scripture helps us in how to respond in a Christlike way to our in-law problems: First, we are to show lifelong honor to our father and mother and to the parents of our spouse. Second, we are also to leave our families and cleave to our spouse, giving our partner first loyalty and devotion. Third, we should apologize to our in-laws if we have wronged them. Fourth, if a confrontation is necessary, the biological child of the in-laws should be the one to speak the truth in love. And fifth, we should make every effort to live at peace. If they won't reciprocate, we are free to move on as Jacob eventually did.

*Heavenly Father, help us to understand the difference between honor and obedience with our parents once we reach adulthood and marry. Amen.*

*Then make my joy complete by being like-
minded, having the same love, being
one in spirit and of one mind.*

PHILIPPIANS 2:2

How can we avoid a misunderstanding in marriage?
An older couple was sitting in the living room
one evening when the phone rang. The wife got up and
answered it in the next room. "It's New York—long distance," she shouted to her husband. Distracted by the television show he was watching, he yelled back, "It sure is.
We drove there last summer."

We all can experience misunderstandings in marriage. A misunderstanding is a failure to comprehend our
spouse's real words, feelings, or intentions. The result is
a conflict driven by the wrong issue. To avoid needless
misunderstandings, try the following: First, stop and give
the other person our undivided attention. Second, repeat
back to them what we just heard them say. Third, ask non-
judgmental questions to clarify their thoughts. And finally,
switch places to allow our spouse to go through the same
process with us.

Once we reach a mutual understanding of the issues
and appreciate our individual perspectives, misunderstandings are all but impossible.

*Dear Jesus, make us like-minded, having
the same love, and being one in spirit
and purpose. Amen.*

*Do two walk together
unless they have agreed to do so?*

Amos 3:3

Does money need to create tensions in marriage? Studies show that money problems are one of the leading causes of divorce. Money, however, does not need to divide a marriage; rather, it can become a point of strength and unity. How can we begin to walk together in agreement regarding our finances?

Let's recognize that God is the owner and we are simply the managers. Let's agree to give at least 10 percent of our total income to God's work and put another 10 percent away in savings as a hedge. Let's formulate a realistic budget that allows for emergencies and allow the more accounting-minded of the two of us to keep the books (though they should be reviewed together regularly). Let us give each partner an equal say over any expenditures that exceed a certain agreed upon amount. Finally, let's never keep secrets about expenditures.

John Wesley gave this wise financial counsel: "Earn as much as you can, save as much as you can, give as much as you can." That advice is money in the bank.

*Lord Jesus, may we share everything we earn,
inherit, or own that we might reflect true
oneness in our marriage. Amen.*

*Keep to a path far from her,*
*do not go near the door of her house,*
*lest you lose your honor to others*
*and your dignity to one who is cruel.*

PROVERBS 5:8-9

Are we building hedges to protect our marriage?
Jerry Jenkins is the author of *Hedges: Loving Your Marriage Enough to Protect It*. He uses the term *hedges* to refer to mutual agreements that we put in place to safeguard our marriage from an affair. He suggests we *never* do the following: Be alone with a member of the opposite sex (absolute privacy leads to absolute intimacy). Meet alone for lunch or other appointments (three is a welcome crowd). Share our emotional issues or problems (or listen to theirs). Compliment their dress, appearance, or figure (mention our spouse's instead). Text, chat online, or develop an Internet relationship (give our spouse all passwords and share the same Facebook page). Engage in intimate eye contact or casual touching (make the hug a tent). And never carpool or travel together alone (take our spouse or another business associate along).

Remember, proper hedges keep fidelity in and intruders out.

*Dear Jesus, make our hedges as high as the*
*ones surrounding Job that the devil*
*complained even he couldn't get through. Amen.*

*Do we not all have one Father? Did not one God*
*create us? Why do we profane the covenant of our*
*ancestors by being unfaithful to one another?*

MALACHI 2:10

Why is it better to stay together than split up?
One common justification for a couple getting
a divorce is, "It's best for everyone involved." We beg to
differ. It's not best for our children—they'll carry the scars
for their lifetime whether they are still at home or grown
up. Neither is it best for our extended family members—
they'll grieve the loss of the people they've come to love.
It's not best for our local church—they'll feel the impact of
our division perhaps for years or decades to come. It's not
best for our community—they'll experience the economic
and social loss of another intact, two-parent family. It's not
best for our health—statistics say we'll live a shorter life
span. It's not best for our future relationships—the statistics for a second marriage failing are higher than for a first.

Now exactly who is the divorce best for?

*Heavenly Father, Your Word says You hate*
*divorce (not divorced people). May we disdain*
*divorce as much as You do. Amen.*

*Dear friends, let us love one another, for
love comes from God. Everyone who loves
has been born of God and knows God.*

1 John 4:7

Why do believers have marriages that last?
Some researchers believe Christians divorce at
the same rate as the society as a whole. That's not entirely
accurate. Couples who report a faith marked by a strong
commitment to the Lordship of Jesus Christ and the
authority of God's Word divorce far less (fewer than 1 percent of couples that daily pray together divorce).

There are reasons committed believers stay together:
They love God more than each other. They believe in the
Bible's original design for marriage. They understand
the dangerous reality of sin. They know true forgiveness
begins at the cross. They experience a oneness that only
the indwelling Christ can provide. The basis of their unity
is found in heaven, not on earth. They accept that perfection exists only in heaven and so forbear with one another.
And they know true love ultimately comes from God and
tap into His limitless supply.

*Dear Jesus, let our marriage be a witness to
the fact we are born of God and know God.
Amen.*

*"This, then, is how you should pray…"*
MATTHEW 6:9

How can the Lord's Prayer protect our marriage? Probably the most well-known prayer found in Scripture is the Lord's Prayer. We believe it can be used to preserve our marriage as each line elicits a confession of faith on our part.

"Our Father in heaven…" We both worship the same loving God. "Hallowed be your name…" We hold You in the highest honor in our marriage. "Your kingdom come, your will be done on earth as it is in heaven…" We are committed to obeying and doing Your will as we understand it. "Give us today our daily bread…" We look to You to provide all our needs each and every day. "Forgive us our debts, as we also have forgiven our debtors…" We turn to You to give us the grace we may lack to forgive each other. "And lead us not into temptation, but deliver us from the evil one…" Your name and Word are all the authority we need to protect us from the devil's schemes.

This is the prayer Jesus taught us to pray.

*Dear Lord and Savior, Yours alone is the*
*kingdom, the power, and the glory*
*forever and ever. Amen.*

*David was greatly distressed because the men*
*were talking of stoning him…But David*
*found strength in the LORD his God.*

1 SAMUEL 30:6

H ow should we respond to a crisis?
Ready or not, crises will someday enter our lives.
For some this means panic, meltdown, blaming, self-pity,
and denial. For others it brings calm, perseverance, trust,
and acceptance. What makes the difference?

Here are several ways to weather unexpected storms
together in a godly fashion: Make our first response to
call out together to God. Always remember we are on
the same team and refuse to turn on each other. However painful the moment, remember crises are often a sign
we're doing something right not wrong. Focus on the truly
important—that is, God and each other—and not necessarily on the urgent. Look to exercise our faith in ways
we have not before. And trust that this crisis is designed
to make our lives more fruitful.

As we find strength in God, we are able to face crises
and emerge stronger for the experience.

*Almighty God, we believe nothing enters our*
*lives that has not first passed through Your*
*sovereign and gracious intentions toward us.*
*Amen.*

*And God is able to make every grace overflow to*
*you, so that in every way, always having everything*
*you need, you may excel in every good work.*

2 CORINTHIANS 9:8 HCSB

How can we be agents of grace to our partner?

Our reactions, not our actions, impact our marriage the most. It's vital we respond with grace when our spouse fails us. Grace takes on a variety of facets in a marriage. In the face of intemperate words, we can decide to show patience. Confronted with criticism, we can choose to compliment our spouse. In the presence of impoliteness, we can choose to display courtesy. Encountering anger, we can choose to offer a gentle answer. Running into judgment and bitterness, we can choose to offer mercy and forgiveness. Experiencing humiliation, we can choose to respond with dignity.

While we should never tolerate wrong behavior, neither should we return like for like. While some issues may need to be confronted, they are far more often resolved when we are responding with an attitude of grace. Grace is the ultimate response that preserves our peace of heart and character.

*Dear Jesus, let grace serve as the final word in*
*all our disagreements. Amen.*

*"Today, if you hear his voice,*
*do not harden your hearts*
*as you did in the rebellion."*

HEBREWS 3:15

How can we keep a soft heart?

The heart is at the heart of all our relationships. Today, if we experience the convicting voice of the Holy Spirit, we must not harden our heart. Scripture offers four steps to a softened heart.

First, ask God to do a thorough heart exam. David prayed, "Search me, God, and know my heart…" (Psalm 139:23). We must give God permission to look deeply into our hearts to find anything offensive to Him. Second, we should admit sin to God and to our spouse, just as James exhorts us, "Confess your sins to each other and pray for each other…" (James 5:16). Such honest admission frees the way for God to cleanse and restore our hearts. Third, invite God to change our heart in any way He chooses. David prayed, "Create in me a pure heart, O God…" (Psalm 51:10). And fourth, forgive those who have offended us. Jesus said, "If you hold anything against anyone, forgive them…" (Mark 11:25). Forgiving others breaks the shackles of bitterness and sets prisoners free— and that's us.

*Lord Jesus, should we hear Your voice today,*
*may we soften our hearts toward You and each*
*other. Amen.*

*Aquila and Priscilla greet you warmly in the Lord,
and so does the church that meets at their house.*

1 Corinthians 16:19

Can a godly home win people to Christ?

We should never underestimate the impact of a Christ-centered marriage on those around us. One such couple of extraordinary influence found in the New Testament was Priscilla and Aquila. These dear friends of the apostle Paul accompanied him on some of his journeys and hosted a church in their home. They were used to mentor Apollos, who later became a powerful spokesman for the gospel.

Why does a godly couple draw others to Christ? A loving marriage is a living object lesson of Christ's love for the church and the church's honor for Christ; it uniquely reveals the glory of Christ; it teaches the future blessings of heaven; it makes an effective prayer life possible; and finally, it makes our testimony credible.

One of the greatest witnesses we can have for Christ is the way we live out our marriage each day.

*Lord, may unbelievers get a glimpse into the
love, warmth, and godliness of a Christian
marriage that will make them envious and
open them to the Good News. Amen.*

*"If someone asks, 'What are these wounds on your body?' they will answer, 'The wounds I was given at the house of my friends.'"*

ZECHARIAH 13:6

What hurts rather than helps a marriage? Certain behaviors may seem quite Christian, but in fact they produce ungodly results. What are these misguided actions? When we take the blame for every problem, we're not being honest; no spouse is always in the wrong. When we believe we deserve to be mistreated; no one ever merits poor treatment—ever. When we excuse our spouse's irresponsible behavior, we are only helping them remain trapped. When we keep our spouse from experiencing the consequences of their sin, we are denying them the motivation to change. When we avoid talking about difficult issues, we guarantee the problems will continue, to everyone's detriment. Finally, when we are afraid to do what's right, we are inadvertently paving the way for our spouse to do wrong.

Speaking the hard truth in love may initially wound, but ultimately it heals.

*Lord Jesus, give us the love to say, do, and live the difficult thing if it is indeed the right thing. Amen.*

*For this is the way the holy women of the past who
put their hope in God used to adorn themselves. They
submitted themselves to their own husbands, like
Sarah, who obeyed Abraham and called him her lord.*

1 PETER 3:5-6

What's wrong with nagging?

Nagging is any attempt to coerce our mate to comply with our wishes by repeatedly making the same request or complaint. While it may succeed in the short term, it ultimately works against building a fulfilling marriage.

Nagging is at base a disrespectful, manipulative, and controlling behavior. No one enjoys being coerced, so as a result, we don't cooperate. Why do spouses still try it? We may feel frustrated or ignored in our attempts to get our spouse's attention or cooperation. Our sinful nature may urge us to turn up the heat. What is the Bible's alternative to nagging? According to Peter, we should put our trust in God and not in our spouse to fulfill our needs. Our submissive and quiet attitude clears the way for God to respond to our honest requests, humble attitudes, and prayerful patience.

*Lord Jesus, help us to ask for what we need in
relationships and then leave the matter with
You. Amen.*

*"I have come that they may have
life, and have it to the full."*

John 10:10

What is the Good News that changes marriages? There is no more powerful instrument for change in a marriage than the gospel of Jesus Christ. Let's start with the fact God loves us—that means He loves both us and our spouse. God has a wonderful plan for our life—that means He also has a wonderful plan for our marriage. Unfortunately sin has separated us from God—sin is also what separates us from our spouse. Thankfully Jesus Christ paid for all our sins—He has also paid for the wrongs we've done against our partner. We can receive Jesus Christ into our life by faith—we can also invite Him into our marriage relationship by faith. Finally, Jesus offers us the gift of eternal life—He also offers the gift of a new start with our spouse.

Have we both taken the step of placing our faith in the finished work of Christ on the cross? Rejoice! We and our marriage are now born again.

*Lord Jesus, this moment we choose to receive
Your free gift of eternal life purchased on the
cross for us. Amen.*

# ABOUT BOB AND CHERYL MOELLER

Bob and Cheryl Moeller are the cofounders of For Better, For Worse, For Keeps Ministries, a ministry dedicated to healing hearts and restoring marriages in underserved communities (www.forkeeps ministries.com).

Bob is the weekly host of a nationally broadcast television call-in show, *Marriage: For Better, For Worse,* on the Total Living Network (www .TLN.com). He also conducts weekend marriage and singles' conferences around the nation. He has been nominated for two Gold Medallion Book Awards and has written articles for such publications as *Focus on the Family, Marriage Partnership*, and *Christianity Today*. Bob holds a doctor of ministry degree from Trinity Evangelical Divinity School.

Cheryl is a seasoned mom, homemaker, conference speaker, and standup comic. She speaks at women's conferences and writing conferences in the Midwest. She's a syndicated columnist (including at www.momlaughs.blogspot.com) and aims to make life a little easier for moms. Cheryl has written for www.mops.org and *Marriage Partnership*. She does comedy for parenting classes, MOPS groups, church retreats, banquets, and those in line at the grocery store.

Bob has been married to his favorite coauthor, Cheryl, for thirty-three years. They have coauthored or written separately fourteen books, five on marriage. They also love to bike, travel, and watch their kids' events. They have six children, one son-in-law, one daughter-in-law, one grandson, and a faithful collie named Bo, who loves everyone he meets.

If you are interested in booking a marriage, singles', or writing conference, you can contact them at: forkeepsministries@gmail.com.

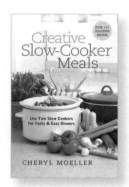

## Creative Slow-Cooker Meals

*Use Two Slow Cookers for Tasty and Easy Dinners*

CHERYL MOELLER

From the coauthor of *One-Minute Devotions for Couples* comes a new kind of cookbook and a new attitude toward planning meals. With an eye toward the whole menu, not just part of it, columnist Cheryl Moeller teaches you to use two crockpots to easily create healthy, homemade dinners.

Don't worry about your dinner being reduced to a mushy stew. Each of the more than 200 recipes has been taste-tested at Cheryl's table. Join the Moeller family as you dig into:

- Salmon and Gingered Carrots
- Mediterranean Rice Pilaf
- Rhubarb Crisp

…and many more! Perfect for the frazzled mom who never has enough time in the day, *Creative Slow-Cooker Meals* gives you more time around the table with delicious, healthy, frugal, and easy meals!